MW00620053

Natural
Wonders
———— *of* ————
Texas

Natural
Wonders
of
Texas

A Guide to
Parks, Preserves
& Wild Places

Paul Cooke and Sunita Cooke
Illustrated by Lois Leonard Stock

Country Roads Press
CASTINE · MAINE

Natural Wonders of Texas:
A Guide to Parks, Preserves & Wild Places
© 1995 by Paul Cooke and Sunita Cooke. All rights reserved.

Published by Country Roads Press
P.O. Box 286, Lower Main Street
Castine, Maine 04421

Text and cover design by Studio 3, Ellsworth, Maine.
Cover photograph courtesy of Leroy Williamson, Texas Parks and
    Wildlife Department.
Illustrations by Lois Leonard Stock.
Typesetting by Typeworks, Belfast, Maine.

ISBN 1-56626-109-0

Library of Congress Cataloging-in-Publication Data

Cooke, Paul, 1961–
    Natural wonders of Texas : a guide to parks, preserves and wild
places / Paul and Sunita Cooke ; illustrator: Lois Leonard Stock.
        p.   cm.
    Includes index.
    ISBN 1-56626-109-0 : $9.95
    1. Texas – Guidebooks.   2. Natural areas – Texas – Guidebooks.
3. Natural history – Texas – Guidebooks.   4. Parks – Texas –
Guidebooks.   5. Botanical gardens – Texas – Guidebooks.
I. Cooke, Sunita.   II. Title.
F384.3.C66   1995
917.6404'63 – dc20   94-32680
                                                                CIP

Printed in the United States of America.
10 9 8 7 6 5 4 3 2 1

*With acknowledgments and thanks to
Andrea Kitay*

Contents

Introduction   *xi*

1 CENTRAL TEXAS
Introduction   *1*
Enchanted Rock State Natural Area   *2*
Hill Country State Natural Area   *6*
Palmetto State Park   *8*
Lost Maples State Natural Area   *13*
Caverns of the Hill Country   *16*
   Natural Bridge Caverns   *17*
   Caverns of Sonora   *18*
   Longhorn Cavern State Park   *20*
   Wonder Cave   *21*
Inks Lake State Park and Inks Dam
     National Fish Hatchery   *22*
Pedernales Falls State Park   *25*

2 WEST TEXAS
Introduction   *28*

Big Bend National Park and Rio Grande
    Wild and Scenic River   29
Big Bend Ranch State Natural Area   35
Guadalupe Mountains National Park   40
Davis Mountains Region   44
    Davis Mountains State Park   45
    Chihuahuan Desert Research Institute   46
    McDonald Observatory   47
    Fort Davis National Historic Site   48
Hueco Tanks State Historical Park   49
Monahans Sandhills State Park   53
Odessa Meteor Crater   55
Seminole Canyon State Historical Park   56

3 SOUTHEAST TEXAS
Introduction   59
Big Thicket National Preserve   62
Roy E. Larson Sandyland Sanctuary   71
Alabama-Coushatta Indian Reservation   74
Martin Dies Jr. State Park and Lake B. A. Steinhagen   76
Brazos Bend State Park   78
The National Forests of Texas   83
    Angelina National Forest   84
    Davy Crockett National Forest   85
    Sabine National Forest   86
    Sam Houston National Forest   87

4 THE UPPER TEXAS COAST
Introduction   89
Sea Rim State Park   92
McFaddin National Wildlife Refuge   95
Anahuac National Wildlife Refuge   96
Galveston Island   99
    Moody Gardens   100

Underwater Adventure 101
Galveston Island State Park 102
Brazosport Area National Wildlife Refuges 103
Brazoria National Wildlife Refuge 105
San Bernard National Wildlife Refuge 107
Aransas National Wildlife Refuge 108

5 **TROPICAL TEXAS**
Introduction 113
Mustang Island State Park 114
Padre Island National Seashore 117
Laguna Atascosa National Wildlife Refuge 122
Santa Ana National Wildlife Refuge 124
Bentsen–Rio Grande Valley State Park 128
Sabal Palm Grove Sanctuary 132

6 **THE PANHANDLE AND NORTH TEXAS**
Introduction 135
Palo Duro Canyon State Park 137
Caprock Canyons State Park 141
Dinosaur Valley State Park 144
Copper Breaks State Park 147
Caddo Lake State Park and
    Wildlife Management Area 149
The National Grasslands of Texas 152
    Rita Blanca National Grassland 154
    Lyndon B. Johnson National Grassland 156
    McClellan Creek National Grassland 158
    Caddo National Grassland 159

Index 161

Introduction

Texas, as those of us who live here know well, is a big, big state, almost 172 million acres. The American Automobile Association estimates that it takes over fifteen hours to drive nonstop from the Louisiana border on the east to El Paso on the west, or from the northern tip of the Panhandle to Brownsville in the south. There are over three million acres of lakes, rivers, and waterways. The Rio Grande River runs for 1,200 miles along the Texas-Mexico border.

But beyond its size, the Texas of the stereotype – dry, dusty, flat, and chock-full of cowboys – is a thing of the imagination. What is real is a state where residents increasingly appreciate the value of existing wilderness areas and the need to protect those that remain.

At present, Texas has 130 state and historical parks and natural areas. There are twelve national-park facilities in Texas, including Padre Island National Seashore, which stretches over 113 miles along the South Texas coast, and Big Bend National Park and Guadalupe Mountains National Park, which preserve unique southwestern ecozones. Thirteen National Wildlife Refuges specifically protect the habitats so vital to wildlife. Four National Forests, four National Grasslands, and five state forests extend the state's wilderness preserves.

Over half of Texas's Gulf Coast is protected in some form by a half-dozen agencies: the National Park Service, U.S. Fish and Wildlife Service, Texas Parks and Wildlife Department, and other county and regional governments. The United Nations has named both the Big Thicket National Preserve and Big Bend National Park as International Biosphere Reserves.

Texas Landscapes

The geology of Texas has shaped this land and its ecosystems. So have its rivers, to a lesser extent: the Pecos, Guadalupe, Rio Grande, Red, Brazos, Colorado, Llano, San Bernard, Trinity, San Antonio, Sabine, and Nueces.

This book divides the state into six unique regions, and devotes a chapter to the parks and wilderness areas in each region: the Central Texas Hill Country, the Trans-Pecos, the Piney Woods of Southeast Texas, the Upper Texas Coast, Tropical Texas and the Rio Grande Valley, and the Panhandle and North Texas—all as varied as they are wide.

Across the state more than 611 different bird species have been recorded, more than 75 percent of all bird species in the United States. Over 140 species of mammals roam the wilds, including mountain lions, ocelots, pronghorn antelope, mountain sheep, alligators, river otters, and dozens of species of snake. From East Texas to West Texas, orchids, rattan, mangroves, oaks, pines, long-stem grasses, cactus, ocotillo, and yucca all reside in their ecological niches.

Economy or Environment?

Texas, like most other states, is torn between economic development and environmental protection, a conflict that has been ongoing since the creation of the National Wildlife Refuge System in 1903, the first effort to preserve habitats for wildlife.

The irrigation needs of Texas farmers and ranchers have led to the impoundment of every major river in Texas. Dams flooded riparian forests, destroyed nesting areas, and drove many species to the brink of extinction. Hunting and habitat destruction further endangered fragile ecosystems and their inhabitants.

Alligators and whooping cranes were endangered but have made a comeback. Not so the indigenous Carolina parakeet, now extinct. The paddlefish and red wolf are endangered and survive only in breeding programs.

But Texans are changing their minds about conservation. In 1983, the Texas legislature created the Special Nongame and Endangered Species Conservation Fund, which provides for the acquisition of wildlife habitats, reestablishment of sea-turtle breeding, and development of education programs.

The U.S. Congress is considering the addition of new lands to the Big Thicket National Preserve, and the 1989 creation of the 264,000-acre Big Bend Ranch State Natural Area (formerly the Diamond A Cattle Company) doubled the size of the state-park system overnight.

Yet even today the Intracoastal Waterway is a main thoroughfare for giant tankers carrying oil and toxic chemicals past fragile salt marshes, where complex ecosystems nurture microorganisms, insects, fish, birds, reptiles, and mammals. And farmers and ranchers continue to convert native grasslands to farms and pasturage.

In the Rio Grande Valley, for example, so much native habitat has been lost, primarily to farming and human development, that rare species like ocelots and jaguarundis are at risk. Happily, local residents are supporting a plan to create a 107,000-acre wildlife corridor along the river, to preserve what remains and restore what is lost.

Despite its many parks, Texas lags behind most other states in the creation of public parkland and wilderness areas. Out of a total land area of 267,338 square miles, fewer than 21,000 square miles, or eight percent, have been set aside for the preservation of wildlife and the enjoyment of the public. But it is a good start.

1

Central Texas

INTRODUCTION

The temperature is never too hot or too cold—by Texas standards—in the Hill Country, miles of rolling limestone plateaus rising to 2,000 feet in elevation, forested with oak and mesquite and dotted with lakes, rivers, recreation reservoirs, parks, and pretty small towns.

That's why the region, northwest of San Antonio and Austin and stretching west to Sonora and Abilene, is probably the most popular and best-known outdoor vacation destination in the state, with wildlife watching, camping, swimming, hiking, horseback riding, rafting, rock climbing, spelunking, and road and mountain biking.

Most of the Hill Country was originally settled by immigrants from Germany, who homesteaded farms and small ranches and built villages that reminded them of home. Today this once rural lifestyle is pumped up by a tourist economy dependent on antiques and craft shops, restaurants, bed-and-breakfasts, and a thriving sports industry, which you can enjoy on your own or with the help of local outfitters.

A network of rivers—the Colorado, Guadalupe, San Antonio, Llano, Pedernales, and Brazos—fed by rainwater, wells, and natural springs, meanders through the hills toward the coastal flatlands, watering lush green valleys and canyons, some of which have been dammed for swimming holes, fishing, canoeing, and river rafting.

Impounded lakes like Lake Travis, outside Austin, permit windsailing, waterskiing, scuba diving, swimming, and fishing and coincidentally provide a habitat for wildlife.

Another famous Hill Country attraction is its limestone caves, complete with stalactites, stalagmites, and other strange formations, scattered throughout Edward's Plateau. The caverns were created when rainwater, percolating through thin topsoil and into the bedrock, dissolved the softer limestone. Some caves, nesting places for Brazilian and Mexican free-tailed bats, contain the world's largest and densest bat populations.

Most roads through the hills are not only scenic but historic, following the routes of horse trails, pioneer wagon tracks, and the old Chisholm Trail, on which cattle were driven north to market towns along the railroad.

Today, the roads provide easy access to places that used to be hard to reach, such as the pink granite domes and cliffs of the Llano uplift at Enchanted Rock, the Hill Country State Natural Area, various recreation lakes, and numerous parks and rivers. The roads' moderate inclines are challenging but not impossible for bicyclers and long-distance runners.

ENCHANTED ROCK STATE NATURAL AREA

If you like rock climbing, hiking, archaeology, or geology, the 1,643-acre Enchanted Rock State Natural Area, in the heart of the Hill Country, just thirty minutes north of Fredericksburg on Ranch Road 965, makes a good weekend destination.

Geology and History

Enchanted Rock was named by Indians who believed the large pink granite domes thrusting upward to the sky were the source of supernatural powers. The granite, a billion years old, was formed when forces deep within the earth superheated the rock, forcing it toward the surface. Before reaching the surface, the magma cooled, creating a hard granite "bubble," a small portion of which has been exposed by erosion and uplift. At night, when the moon is up in a cloudless sky, the distinctively rounded pink crystalline rock gleams and sparkles.

A number of ancient archaeological sites found throughout the park indicate that early man lived in the area for 8,000 years, spanning the Paleo-Indian, Pre-Archaic, and Archaic periods. The late Prehistoric period began around A.D. 900, when Indian pottery and arrowheads were fashioned as tools. Indian villages and camping places have been identified on stream banks, among the rock formations, and along trails in Enchanted Rock.

These ancient peoples were followed by a tribe known as the Tonkawa, and later by the Comanche and Apache, all of whom were forced out of the area before 1800. The Enchanted Rock park headquarters has a small but detailed exhibit of the area's human history, and sells books on history and archaeology.

Rock Climbing

Rock climbing on "the big pink bubble" is one of the great recreational attractions for both novice and experienced climbers. Hard granite, a rock that rarely flakes or shatters, is rare in Texas, but at Enchanted Rock it rises hundreds of feet in vertical spires and mounts, cut by deep clefts.

Rock-climbing clubs come from as far as Dallas and Houston for weekend climbs and novice classes. To join a class or organize one, contact any sports store selling climbing equipment.

Climbers are required to check in at park headquarters before starting out, should have some prior climbing experience, and are expected to use ropes for safety. Pitons, bolts, and other hardware that defaces the rock surface are not allowed. Park rangers can advise you on the locations of various routes and the degree of difficulty, measured from 5.0 (scrambling conditions) to 5.12 (hanging upside-down by your fingertips).

Hiking and Backpacking

A more leisurely way to see Enchanted Rock is along the four-mile hiking trail that loops around the rock's base, an easy, meandering trail with no elevation gain that passes several back-country camping sites. Avoid leaving the trail, since the soil is prone to erosion. Canopied benches are located near the trailhead for a break from the hot sun, but you should always carry plenty of water.

The hike to the top of Enchanted Rock is short and quick, a 0.6-mile trudge that introduces you to one of the more unusual ecosystems in the park. On the flat summit are many shallow depressions called *vernal pools*, where specialized plant and animal forms survive in a dormant condition from one season to the next. During the dry season, fairy-shrimp eggs lie dormant, waiting for rain. When the rains come and the hollows fill with water, the eggs hatch, the young grow to adults, new eggs are laid, and the cycle continues as the pools dry up, all within a few days. Pick up a pamphlet describing this ecosystem from park headquarters before you start up on the trail.

Backpacking is also very popular here. The Moss Lake and Walnut Spring Primitive Camping Areas are about a mile down the Echo Canyon Trail, which winds between Enchanted Rock and its lower neighbor, Little Rock. Both sites are also accessible by hiking two miles from the parking area on the Loop Trail.

The Buzzard's Roost Primitive Camping Area, popular with rock climbers, is about two miles from the trailhead, off the Loop Trail and a cutoff to the bottom of Buzzard's Roost.

Wildlife viewing in this part of the park is limited to armadillos, deer, and squirrels, although campers may be lucky enough to catch glimpses of coyotes and bobcats at night.

Where: Thirty minutes north of Fredericksburg on Ranch Road 965. Follow the signs to the entrance.
Hours: Open daily year-round.
Admission: Nominal entrance and camping fee.
Best time to visit: March to May and September to November. The summer sun can heat the rock, making hiking and climbing difficult. In the winter, the weather varies dramatically from 30° to 70° F.
Activities: Backpacking, rock climbing, camping, archaeology, hiking, and wildlife viewing.
Concessions: None. The nearest stores are in Fredericksburg.
Other: Walk-in camping only. This is one of the most popular outdoor destinations in the Hill Country. The nearest accommodations are in Fredericksburg. Do not pitch tents in low-lying areas due to risk of flash floods. Ground fires are not permitted: bring a camp stove. Carry extra water on all hikes. Check with park headquarters for rock-climbing rules and routes.
For more information:
Park Superintendent, Enchanted Rock State Natural Area, Route 4, Box 170, Fredericksburg, TX 78642; 915-247-3903.

HILL COUNTRY STATE NATURAL AREA

The Hill Country State Natural Area, 5,400 acres of undeveloped, rolling countryside, is a haven for backcountry adventure. Horseback riding, mountain biking, backpacking, hiking, and wildlife viewing are popular activities in this secluded wilderness west of San Antonio. The state has protected the area for the enjoyment of recreationists but has no plans for developing the natural area into a park. Locals hope that the preserve doesn't become too popular and that it remains their special secret.

Bicycling

Unlike some other parks in Texas, this natural area allows mountain biking on backcountry trails. Portions of the trails track through streams and along some steep cliffs, paths so narrow that even top-class riders generally get off and walk. Trail conditions change quickly, so watch your speed and wear protective equipment. Unexpected rocks, muddy streambeds, and trees pop up around most corners. Always carry extra water; the water in the natural area is not drinkable.

Hiking

This park also contains some of the most remote hiking areas in central Texas, with thirteen trails winding over thirty-two miles through the hills and steep valleys and along creeks. In some places the hills rise 600 feet over steep, stream-cut ravines. Cross-country bushwhacking is possible, but be sure to pick up a free topographic map from the visitors center first, and be prepared for thick brush.

Day hikers like the Bandera Creek Trail, an easy four-mile

round-trip walk along a rocky seasonal streambed. For a more challenging route, hike to the top of Cougar Canyon on the Twin Peaks Saddleback Trail and the Cougar Canyon Overlook Trail. This seven-mile round-trip trail climbs a steep grade near the top of the canyon. The rangers ask that you stay on the established path to minimize erosion.

Camping, Backpacking, Horseback Riding

Two long trails, not only for hikers but also for horseback riders, are popular with equestrians from Austin, San Antonio, and Waco, who trailer their animals in for the weekend. Three campgrounds are accessible by car; another three can be reached only on foot or by horse. The nearest is only 1.5 miles from the trailhead, an easy destination for most weekenders. Flies and mosquitoes can be a problem, so bring insect repellent. On the trails, horses always have the right of way, followed by hikers and then mountain bikers.

Strict park regulations are designed to minimize human impact on the wilderness. Camping is permitted in designated areas only, and campfires must be in established fire rings. The risk of forest fire in this arid climate is highest from May through October. No drinking water is available in the backcountry, so carry what you'll need.

Wildlife

Out in the backcountry, shrubs rustle as wild turkeys forage and deer graze in the underbrush. Red-tailed hawks and vultures circle above, waiting for a meal. Rattlesnakes hide from predators and the sun's heat in the undergrowth and in rock crevices. At night, the constellations, undimmed by city lights, fill the night sky, and the yipping of coyotes punctuates the silence.

Where: Almost due west of San Antonio. Follow State 173 south to Ranch Road 1077 and signs to the park.
Hours: Open year-round.
Admission: Nominal entrance fee.
Best time to visit: September to May.
Activities: Backpacking, hiking, horseback riding, mountain biking, primitive backpack and car camping, and limited wildlife viewing.
Concessions: None.
Pets: Dogs must be kept on a leash and under supervision. Horses cannot be left unattended at any time. Pack in what hay you will need and pack out what you don't use.
Other: The park trails are open to bikers, hikers, and horseback riders. Follow trail etiquette. Ground fires in camp are prohibited. Be conscientious about pollution and noise while in this primitive wilderness area.
For more information:

Hill Country State Natural Area, Route 1, Box 601, Bandera, TX 78003; 512-796-4413.

PALMETTO STATE PARK

Palmetto State Park, nestled in the rust-colored, oak-covered, rolling hills east of San Antonio, protects the Ottine Swamp, a small vestige of southeastern U.S. swampland isolated in dry ore-laden hills. This 268-acre park is named after the dwarf palmetto, a short palm-like plant with large, spiked, green fronds that grows in well-watered soils, the last survivor of a swamp that flourished here more than 12,000 years ago.

For sixty years, the park's hot spring–fed bogs have been threatened by increasingly arid weather and a decrease in the flow of ground water, which has been pumped out to irrigate nearby farms. To counteract the loss, in 1934 the Civilian Conservation Corp. built a water tower, an artesian well, and a ramjet hydraulic pump in the park. Today, rangers at the park headquarters believe that without the CCC project, the bogs that support the large stands of dwarf palmettos would have dried up years ago.

This park is replete with scenery, opportunities to raft and canoe, and chances for serious birders to increase their counts.

Scenic Drives

To find your way into the park, take US 183 south off I-10 and follow the signs to Park Road 11. Note how oxidized metal in the soil has turned the earth a rich orange-brown. From the scenic overlook you can survey the valley where jungle swamps once stretched to the horizon and where today most of the land is tilled for agriculture.

As the road descends into the valley where the San Marcos River makes its way toward the Gulf, large oaks covered with draperies of Spanish moss arch overhead, blocking out the sun. Stop in Ottine, at the small park's visitors center, for information and camping permits. Further on, Park Road 11 leads to the park's two entrances.

The first road enters the park on the left where an oxbow lake curves around and underneath the road. Here you will find campgrounds and a bubbling natural sulfur hot spring that trickles down into the lake. To get to the second entrance, continue driving south over the oxbow lake, cross over the deep ravine of the San Marcos River, which runs through the park, and look for the signs indicating an entrance on your left. From the second road, watch for signs to the trailheads, picnic shelter, and more campgrounds.

Hiking and Canoeing

Visitors can raft, swim, and fish in the San Marcos. Naturalists like bird-watching and hiking the park's four maintained trails. Paddlers enjoy canoeing through the reeds near the shore on the oxbow lake. If you have your own inner tube, you can raft on the peaceful and quiet San Marcos River.

The Lake Trail, River Trail, Palmetto Trail, and Hiking Trail combine to make up roughly three miles of maintained nature paths. In summer, however, the forest swelters under the sun and humidity, making all but the shaded Palmetto Trail unbearable. Fortunately, the latter happens to be the most interesting, winding through thick palmetto groves and swamps. Pick up an interpretive trail guide at the trailhead and set out.

On either side of the trail, small mosquito fish populate the ponds and swamps. The fish feed on the thriving mosquito larvae (bring insect repellent). While following the guide, look for the willow trees, palmetto groves, ash, elder, cedar, and tall sycamores. Search for the bright red flowers of the trumpet creeper vine, and with luck, you may see a ruby-throated hummingbird.

The River Trail is the longest in the small park at 1.25 miles. The trail guide says the state tree (a pecan tree) found at sign marker number 2 rises over 100 feet tall and is a member of the walnut hardwood family. Ferns and other swamp flora thrive along the river's edge.

The bluffs along the river are unstable, so don't get too close to the edge. Near marker number 5, note the gray, lacy Spanish moss, a relative of the pineapple, hanging from the trees. Heading back along the loop trail through the forest, watch out for enormous spider webs, up to six feet in diameter, that block the path. They are very photogenic in early morning before the dew has evaporated.

Wildlife

The Texas Parks and Wildlife Department has had a running problem with snakes in the park. At night, rattlers and cotton-mouth water moccasins emerge from the shaded brush onto roads and concrete paths for warmth. Be especially careful around the edges of the oxbow lake and the sulfur springs, where snakes often rest in the tall, cool grass.

Shy, nocturnal flying squirrels glide rather than fly

Along with the snakes come a host of less dangerous wildlife. Deer are often spotted grazing in the forest while bobcats stalk squirrels, mice, and rabbits at night. Occasionally, flying squirrels can be seen overhead, navigating the airways between the treetops.

A bird checklist maintained by the Parks and Wildlife Department names 275 different species, a third more than the count in nearby parks, a testament to the biodiversity of Palmetto State Park's swampland. With little effort it is possible to spot up to twenty different species on any given day.

The ranger slide show given on weekend evenings at the picnic shelter is a good way to relax after a long day hiking. The picnic shelter, built by the CCC during the 1930s, once sported a dwarf-palmetto thatched roof, but today a wood roof protects you from the wind and rain.

Where: About sixty miles east of San Antonio. Go south from I-10 on US 183 toward Ottine. Follow the signs to the park headquarters and entrances.

Hours: Open year-round for day visitors and campers.

Admission: Nominal entrance and camping fee. For camping and entrance permits, stop by the park headquarters, which is located north of the entrance in Luling.

Best time to visit: March to May and September to November.

Activities: Hiking, camping, swimming, rafting, canoeing, birdwatching, fishing, wildlife identification, picnicking, and educational programs.

Concessions: None. The nearby town of Luling has stores and a restaurant.

Pets: Must always be on a leash.

Other: Slide shows are given by the park staff on summer Saturday evenings at the picnic shelter. Visit the old post-office building in the nearby town of Luling. The wooden building has served as the post office since the days when this was a frontier town.

For more information:

Park Superintendent, Palmetto State Park, Route 5, Box 201, Gonzales, TX 78629; 512-672-3266.

LOST MAPLES STATE NATURAL AREA

The Lost Maples State Natural Area encompasses 2,173 acres of forested canyon lands through which the Sabinal River flows. The river brings water to thick groves of bigtooth maples, trees that have survived here since prehistoric times.

The first grove of maples thrived in the canyon bottom at least 10,000 years ago, when the climate was similar and mastodons, saber-toothed tigers, and giant bison roamed the groves. Today, other trees flourish in the fertile soil along the riverbanks as well: oaks, walnuts, and sycamores.

The Maple Trees

The maple trees, stranded in the canyon thousands of years ago when the last great global warming period began and the ice sheets covering North America began to recede, have survived in this moist pocket of central Texas. Unlike most other flora, which disappeared as the climate dried out, the maples are now found only here, protected by their location in deep valleys, and in large stands hundreds of miles to the west and north.

To protect the existing maples from the damaging embrace of too many human admirers, rangers have placed restrictions on the number of campgrounds, visitor facilities, and licensed concessionaires, all to limit attendance in the park. The exception occurs in mid-October, when sudden cold temperatures cause the leaves to change color, attracting thousands of day-trippers out for the annual fall display of red, burgundy, yellow, and orange leaves.

Plants and Wildlife

Oaks, walnuts, junipers, and 350 other plant species create a habitat for a diverse avian community, from warblers to raptors.

**Golden eagles soar on great wide wings,
searching for rabbits and rodents**

Bald and golden eagles are regularly seen above Sabinal Canyon, while the woodlands on the canyon floor are home to the endangered golden-cheeked warbler and other birds. A bird checklist, listing over 110 species, is available at the visitors center.

While you're there, ask for reports of recent mountain-lion sightings. The big cats are occasional nocturnal visitors here. More common and just as interesting are bobcats, ringtails, and javelinas. Other unusual creatures are the barking and cliff frogs, both elusive and rarely spotted. Rare plant species found in the park include the Texas barberry and the Canada moonseed.

Hiking

Ten miles of foot trails lead to eight primitive camping areas, the closest site being just 1.5 miles from the trailhead. Backcountry campsites are located along the trails, near streams, and up higher on the drier slopes. Car campsites are also available.

If your stay is a short one, walk the interpretive Maple Trail, only a half-mile walk, but well worth the time. The trail passes through stands of ancient maples and sycamores that seem out of place here in central Texas. The longest trail in the park, a 7.7-mile calorie-burning hike, begins along the East Trail and loops back around on the West Trail, a route better suited to endurance athletes. Take plenty of water.

Several shorter hikes off the East and West Trails take you to overlooks and camping sites without water or facilities. During the summer, hikers can relax next to the cool waters of the Sabinal River or eat lunch under the magnificent forest canopy at Can Creek.

Before leaving, visit the small interpretive center at park headquarters. Here learn about the Native American inhabitants of long ago and where in the canyon they once lived.

Where: The park is located four miles north of the town of Vanderpool on Ranch Road 187. From Bandera follow State 16 west, then pick up Ranch Road 470 to Ranch Road 187. Follow the signs to the park entrance.

Hours: The park is open daily. Call ahead for campsite availability. The park headquarters is open from 8:00 A.M. to 5:00 P.M.

Admission: Nominal entrance and camping fees.

Best time to visit: February to June and September to November.

Activities: Hiking, backpacking, bicycling, bird-watching, swimming, fishing, camping, picnicking, and watching the turning of the fall foliage.

Concessions: None in the park.

Pets: Permitted only on a leash.

Other: After October the rangers begin providing telephone updates on the color of the fall maple foliage. Primitive camping requires permits from park headquarters. The campsites are rarely full, except during October. Ground fires are prohibited.

For more information:

Park Superintendent, Lost Maples State Natural Area, HC01, Box 156, Vanderpool, TX 78885; 512-966-3413.

CAVERNS OF THE HILL COUNTRY

The story of the immense caverns of the Hill Country begins between 66 and 144 million years ago in deep ocean water, where plants, shellfish, fish, and microscopic organisms thrived in a rich environment.

As thousands of years came and went, the ocean floor was layered thick with the remains of sea life. Then, 5 to 10 million years ago, the ocean receded and the bottom was gradually uplifted over 2,000 feet above sea level, creating the Edward's

Plateau and its aquifer, which was gradually overlaid with a layer of dirt deposited by blowing winds, the rich soils in which post oaks and mesquite thrive.

Gradually, rain and wind eroded the Edward's uplift, sculpting rolling hills and winding river canyons. As water trickled through the ancient limestone, it created cavities and calcium deposits, eventually flowing through cracks and crevices down to the Edward's aquifer and opening up vast underground caverns.

Most of the caves known today were discovered years ago by ranchers drilling for water or when they noticed flights of bats emerging from holes in the earth. Although scientists think that hundreds of caves are still undiscovered, the most spectacular have now been designated as National Natural Landmarks and are thus protected, even though most are on private land. In 1932, one cave and the surrounding land were set aside as Longhorn Cavern State Park.

Natural Bridge Caverns

Natural Bridge Caverns, named for the sixty-foot limestone span arching over the deep cut that descends to the cave entrance, are the single most visited cavern system in Texas. Tours lead groups through the privately owned caves on a narrow path, which descends over 100 feet below the surface.

As rainwater seeping through the earth's surface falls from the ceiling on your shoulders, guides explain the "birth of a living cave." Drops seeping downward slowly erode the limestone, cutting and molding all the formations. As calcium carbonate leaches from the limestone and is redeposited on cave walls, floors, and ceilings, it creates fantastically shaped stalagmites, which rise from the floor of the cave, and stalactites, which hang from the ceiling. The caverns' tallest formation, the fifty-foot Watchtower column, was created when a stalactite and a stalagmite met and joined. The crystals shine and glisten in the colored electric lights.

As you pass above Purgatory Creek, gurgling an apparently heart-stopping 100 feet below you, the guide points out the optical illusion and explains that the creek is really only twenty or thirty feet away. For a moment, as the guide switches off the electricity and turns on a flashlight, you imagine the thrill of being the first explorer to see the cave. But flickering shapes and shadows and illusions of distance remind you that spelunking is a sport best enjoyed by those immune to vertigo and claustrophobia.

Where: From I-35, between New Braunfels and San Antonio, follow FM 3009 for thirty minutes west. Signs will lead you to the entrance.

Hours: Open daily, except holidays. Tours enter the cave every few minutes throughout the day.

Admission: Nominal fee for the seventy-five-minute tour through the caverns.

Concessions: The owners of the caverns have built a gaudy gift shop near the entrance. The adjacent restaurant is very expensive and not very good.

For more information:
    Natural Bridge Caverns, 210-657-6101.

Caverns of Sonora

The Caverns of Sonora, located on the far west side of the Hill Country, have the world's largest number of two strange and rare formations, helictites and soda straws, which cover the walls and ceilings of entire rooms.

The helictites are hollow tubes, smaller in diameter than a pencil, formed when water seeps so slowly through a channel that when it emerges at the opening it dries without dripping, leaving a calcium deposit. The helictites covering the walls and ceilings grow irregularly in random directions, dependent on gravity and uneven drying of the deposits. Ask your guide to point out a unique butterfly formation created by two fishtail helictites.

Soda straws, similar to helictites, are formed in a similar manner, except that they hang vertically from the ceiling in long, thin tubes. Because some soda straws are several feet long with side walls no thicker than a sixty-fourth of an inch, the guides ask you to move quietly past, avoiding loud noises.

Over 95 percent of the caverns are alive and still forming as surface water percolates downward. Geologists, who study the stalactites, stalagmites, cave coral, fishtails, helictites, ribbons, and soda straws, estimate this cave to be about sixty million years old.

Nearly all formations in the caverns are pure white calcium carbonate, but some look a little like fried bacon because of small amounts of naturally occurring reddish iron oxide. Some cave pools have a greenish color because visitors throw copper pennies into the water, but others are so clear it's hard to tell where the water's surface meets the rock.

Guided tours descend to a depth of 150 feet, exploring only 1.5 miles of the known 7.5 miles of caverns. Professional spelunkers, however, have explored the cave to a depth of 175 feet. Of the portion explored, over 95 percent is still forming.

As you enter the cave's outer chamber, guides point out places that are black in color and no longer "living," despoiled by oil and dirt on the hands of human explorers. In addition, the increasingly arid climate has dried out some rooms near the surface, making this portion of the caverns the least interesting.

Don't rush during your tour, since even mild exertion in the warm, humid air is tiring. Temperatures in the cave remain at a constant 71°F with a humidity of 98 percent.

Campgrounds, convenient for visitors traveling east-west

on I-10 between Fort Stockton and Junction, are located near the entrance to the caves. Hookups are available.

Where: The caves are a twenty-minute drive south from Sonora, off I-10. Follow signs to the entrance.
Hours: Daily, except holidays. Summer hours are 8:00 A.M. to 6:00 P.M.; winter hours are 9:00 A.M. to 5:00 P.M.
Admission: Nominal fee to tour the caverns, a separate fee to camp.
Concessions: The property owners operate a coffee and gift shop. A small amphitheater has outdoor entertainment and barbecues on summer afternoons and evenings.
For more information:
The Caverns of Sonora, 915-387-2880.

Longhorn Cavern State Park

Longhorn Cavern is not only a geologic attraction but a historic one as well, since it was used as a Confederate fortress during the Civil War. For this reason the Texas Department of Parks and Wildlife has designated this a state park. The rolling, wooded hills around the entrance to the caves are used by hikers and picnickers out for a weekend of relaxation.

The principal attraction of the park, the caves, descend over a half mile into the earth, but visitors walk through only a portion on a 1.25-mile loop trail.

The tour begins in a small room with tower formations, called Crystal City, and proceeds deeper into the cave past the Queen's Throne. In an hour or so, you pass through a succession of connected rooms, including the Viking's Prow, Hall of Gems, Giant Icicle, Frozen Waterfall, Attic, and Lumbago Alley.

After your tour, visit the park headquarters to learn about the Confederate Army's use of the cavern to manufacture gunpowder, and how the caverns also served as a dance hall and restaurant. Archaeologists have even unearthed evidence indicating the cavern was used by ancient Indian tribes for shelter.

Where: Off US 281, between Burnet and Marble Falls.
Hours: Open daily for tours year-round. Spring, fall, and winter hours are 10:00 A.M. to 5:00 P.M.; summer hours are 10:00 A.M. to 6:00 P.M.
Admission: Nominal entrance fee.
Activities: Hiking, spelunking, and picnicking.
Concessions: Gift and snack shops are near the entrance.
For more information:
     Park Superintendent, Longhorn Cavern State Park, Route 2, Box 23, Burnet, TX 78611; 512-756-6976.

Wonder Cave

According to local legend, Wonder Cave was discovered by the wife of a cattle rancher who was drilling for water and lost his drill bit, a very expensive item. Annoyed and determined to find it, he searched in the place where the bit had disappeared and found a large hole. His wife agreed to be lowered through the hole on a rope and discovered the cave.

     Strangely enough, however, Wonder Cave was not formed by water percolating through a limestone bed. Instead, geologists believe that the cave is on the fault line that separates Edward's Plateau from the coastal plains. During cataclysmic geologic movement of Edward's Plateau, large stones became wedged in between two plates, holding them far enough apart to create the cave.

     Only one small formation indicates that Wonder Cave was ever "alive." This is a small flowstone where seeping water deposited calcium in a "flowing" formation. Long ago, however, the oils and acids from the hands of visitors turned the flow black.

The forty-five-minute exploration starts inside a building constructed over the cave entrance and descends deep into the cave, where the guide asks you to sit on a stone bench while the lights are switched off momentarily, revealing complete darkness. Then black lights come on, revealing minerals that glow green and purple.

Wonder Cave has none of the spectacular formations found in living caves, but it is no less a thrill to walk deep in the earth along an earthquake fault and imagine the power that uplifted all of the Hill Country.

Where: Wonder Cave is a well-advertised destination. It lies fifteen minutes south of Austin, west off I-35.

Hours: During the summer, the cave is open from 8:00 A.M. to 8:00 P.M. In the fall, winter, and spring, it is open from 9:00 A.M. to 6:00 P.M.

Admission: The entrance fee to the cave is stiff, at $10.50.

Concessions: A café and gift shop have been built over the entrance to Wonder Cave, a marketing gimmick, since in order to tour the cave you have to stand around the shop waiting for the tour to depart.

For more information:

Wonder Cave, 512-396-8900.

INKS LAKE STATE PARK
and INKS DAM NATIONAL FISH HATCHERY

Inks Lake State Park, on the shore of 803-acre Inks Lake in the Llano uplift region, is ringed by pink granite—the same stone used to build the capitol in Austin. For many visitors, the 1,200-acre park is a pleasant, centrally located jumping-off point for trips to Longhorn Caverns, Enchanted Rock, and Pedernales Falls State Park. But for some curious folks, it has another, stranger attraction: the Inks Dam National Fish Hatchery, where paddlefish are raised.

The U.S. Fish and Wildlife Service, which manages the hatchery to stock lakes and streams throughout the Southwest, raises the paddlefish from fingerlings, but keeps specimens of all ages in various pools, including a number of mature paddlefish, used for breeding.

The paddlefish, which local anglers call "spoonbill cats," are peculiar critters that grow to about six feet in length and weigh upwards of fifty pounds, and have long paddle-like noses, large toothless jaws, and bluish-green skin. Their nearest living relative is the Chinese paddlefish found in the Yangtze River basin in China, but it is also a freshwater relative of the sturgeon.

Biologists aren't actually sure about the purpose of the paddle, but one hypothesis states that the fish uses it to detect concentrations of zooplankton, which are then passed through gill rakers and filtered from the water.

Biologists at Texas A&M University and the Texas Parks and Wildlife Department are studying the paddlefish, hoping to reestablish a stable population in the state's waterways. Fortunately, most fishermen are more interested in Inks Lake's bass population, and would rather not hook a paddlefish, whose cartilaginous skeleton is hard both to clean and to filet. In fact, purposely catching and keeping one would not only net you one of North America's largest freshwater specimens, but an equally large penalty for catching an endangered species.

The real threat to the paddlefish has been the disappearance of its breeding grounds and migration corridors, which have shrunk steadily since water impoundment projects started in Texas. The dams prevent the migratory paddlefish from returning to their native spawning grounds. Present conservation efforts are directed at maintaining a healthy gene pool at this and other fisheries, to help ensure the species' survival.

Inks Lake is also a favorite scuba-diving location, with

better visibility than there is at most other central Texas lakes. During summer, student divers train near the shoreline and take their open-water certification dives with expert dive masters in deeper water. Telltale bubbles seen breaking the water's surface and a stationary dive buoy are signals for boats to avoid the area. Dive shops in nearby Austin and even as far away as Dallas, San Antonio, and Houston can arrange trips to Inks Lake for novice divers as well as experienced divers taking a refresher course.

There are 7.5 miles of hiking trails in Inks Lake State Park. Backpackers can hike to primitive campsites a mile from park headquarters. Hiking trails cross juniper and mesquite woodlands, and you may spot deer, turkeys, and squirrels along the trail.

Car camping is allowed along the lakeshore near the park entrance. The park has two fishing piers and several fish-cleaning houses. Ask at the park headquarters for directions to the boat ramp.

Where: The state park is three miles south of State 29 between Burnet and Llano, where the Colorado River is dammed to form Inks Lake. Follow Park Road 4 to the entrance. The Inks Dam National Fish Hatchery is three miles farther on Park Road 4.
Hours: Open daily year-round.
Admission: Nominal entrance and camping fees.
Best time to visit: March to June and September to November.
Activities: Hiking, camping, fishing, backpacking, scuba diving, boating, and bird-watching.
Pets: Must be kept on a leash.
Other: Many visitors use Inks Lake as a base to visit other parks and natural areas in the Hill Country.
For more information:
Park Superintendent, Inks Lake State Park, Route 2, Box 31, Burnet, TX 78611; 512-793-2223.

Inks Dam National Fish Hatchery, Route 2, Burnet, TX 78611; 512-793-2474.

PEDERNALES FALLS STATE PARK

This semi-arid park is named after the Pedernales Falls, but there really aren't any falls to speak of in the vicinity. But in places, the Pedernales River does emerge from its worn channel to flow in ripples across a series of mildly tilted limestone slabs.

Smaller, vertical, more traditional waterfalls form where tributaries and creeks flow through narrow cuts in the land, converging with the river. These canyons support lush, green, almost tropical plant life, a strange phenomenon in this dry landscape. As you might expect, local bird and animal life centers around these smaller canyons and along the river's edge. Visitors can mountain bike, backpack, hike, swim in the river, or angle for catfish and bass.

The road to the 4,860-acre park, a fifteen-minute drive east of Johnson City and forty-five minutes west of Austin, crosses dry, gently rolling limestone hills. From the entrance station and parking area, you can walk a short way down the hill and picnic at the falls.

Hiking

Start with a short walk on the quarter-mile interpretive loop trail, the Pedernales Hill Country Nature Trail, using the trail guide available at park headquarters. The guide introduces you to the area's ecology and geology and points out common desert plants—the prickly pear and yucca—that thrive in the dry, sandy soil. As you explore you'll find that the park is a series of oases in a semi-arid environment, with shade trees and ferns surrounding clear pools.

The moderately difficult seven-mile Wolf Trail winds through oak and mesquite wilderness. A backcountry campsite is located along the trail about two miles from the trailhead. Stop for lunch at Arrowhead Pool, where a small waterfall feeds this pristine oasis. Overhanging tree branches support a gallery of chirping birds, including (on occasion) the golden-cheeked warbler.

A four-mile-long, tough trek, the Loop Trail is for conditioned hikers only. The trail crosses the river at Trammels Crossing and climbs the rise on the east side of the river to a plateau. The path is largely unshaded from the sun and very steep in places.

Bicycling

Mountain biking is popular, but demanding, since the hills are steep and there are a number of small canyons and ridges. Hikers have the right of way on trails but need to watch for mountain bikers anyway. Since most trails are long and rocky, bikers should take an extra tube, changing kit, and a second bottle of water. More than one biker on this trail has had to carry the bike back to the car. The most popular biking trails are the Loop Trail and the Wolf Mountain Trail, to the top of Wolf Mountain.

Wildlife

Small canyons, secluded pools, creeks, and the river make this park a natural habitat for wildlife. Wild turkeys, deer, snakes, and a variety of birds, including kingfishers and golden eagles, are native to this area. The *Audubon Society Field Guide to North*

American Birds: Eastern Region is a good supplement to the bird checklist available at park headquarters.

A very small visitors center near the park entrance displays a few examples of petrified wood, fossils, and rocks found in the park. Take a peek before leaving.

The shallow valley through which the Pedernales runs fills rapidly after rains, and the area is prone to flash floods. *Be sure to avoid low-lying areas after rains.* The park rangers sound early-warning sirens to alert campers, hikers, and day visitors whenever there is a risk of flooding.

If you hear the siren, *drop everything and climb to the nearest high ground.* Don't be deceived by good weather, because flash floods can be caused by heavy downpours miles away.

Where: Nine miles east of Johnson City on FM 2766. Or drive thirty-two miles west of Austin on US 290 and turn north for six miles on FM 3232.

Hours: Open daily.

Admission: Nominal entrance and camping fee.

Best time to visit: February to June and September to November. The park is a nice destination during warm winter days.

Activities: Swimming, fishing, camping, hiking, mountain biking, backpacking, and picnicking.

Pets: Allowed only on a leash.

Other: Both backcountry and drive-in campsites are available. Ask at the park headquarters about the early-warning alerts for floods.

For more information:

Park Superintendent, Pedernales Falls State Park, Route 1, Box 450, Johnson City, TX 78636; 512-868-7302.

2

West Texas

INTRODUCTION

Miles of gently curving highways, herds of wild pronghorn ante-lope, rolling grasslands, rocky mountains, and stark Chihuahuan desert — this is remote West Texas, the state's driest and least pop-ulated region. West Texas fits the Texas stereotype: tall buttes, sixty-mile visibility, large cattle ranches, and cloudless skies.

In the north, the land shifts slowly from forested high mountains over 8,000 feet in elevation, to rolling grasslands at 4,000 to 5,000 feet, and finally down to Chihuahuan desert at 2,000 to 4,000 feet above sea level. Average elevations between 3,000 and 5,000 feet lend the area around the Guadalupe and Davis Mountains some of Texas's most tolerable year-round weather. These mountain ranges divide the oil-rich Toyah-Permian basin in the east from the low, rolling plains and El Paso in the west.

To the south is Big Bend country. The grasslands around Fort Stockton and Alpine slope gently downward toward Big Bend National Park and the Rio Grande Wild and Scenic River, the border with Mexico. As the average elevation drops from 5,000 feet to below 2,000 feet, the characteristic vegetation of the Chihuahuan desert takes over. Ocotillo, cactus, and thin grasses cover the increasingly arid, featureless landscape. The silhouettes of mountain ranges rise on the horizon.

Though isolated, West Texas has some of the most scenic natural wonders in the state, including the Odessa Meteor Crater, Hueco Tanks State Historical Park, Monahans Sandhills State Park, the Davis Mountains, and Seminole Canyon State Historical Park. The state's only two national parks, Big Bend National Park and Guadalupe Mountains National Park, are here also, as are the Rio Grande Wild and Scenic River area and the Big Bend Ranch State Natural Area, the largest state park in Texas.

BIG BEND NATIONAL PARK
and RIO GRANDE WILD AND SCENIC RIVER

Big Bend National Park is nestled in a giant bend of the Rio Grande, where the river flows southeast and then turns to make a broad swing northward. With over 800,000 acres of Chihuahuan desert and 7,000-foot mountains, the park stretches for 107 miles along the Rio Grande and Mexico. An additional 127 miles of river beginning at the eastern border of the park and another 9,600 acres downstream are designated as the Rio Grande Wild and Scenic River Area.

Before you get to the park, decide what you want to see and do here. With 234 miles of river, 110 miles of paved roads, and over 150 miles of unimproved roads, you won't be able to see everything. Possible activities range from river rafting, which is how we first discovered the area, to hiking, backcountry camping, mountain and road biking, bird-watching, educational seminars on desert life, scenic drives, fishing, horseback riding, and nature photography.

History

Big Bend National Park is still both primitive and remote. It wasn't until 1987 that private phone lines replaced public pay phones in the nearby almost-ghost town of Terlingua and the villages of Lajitas and Study Butte. The nearest commercial airport is in Midland, over 250 miles away, or you can arrange a charter flight to Alpine, 109 miles from the park, and rent a car. The nearest doctor is in Alpine, or over the border in the Mexican city of Ojinaga.

Only three paved roads enter the park. Ranch Road 170 on the west comes from Ojinaga in Chihuahua, Mexico. US 385 comes from Marathon, and US 118 from Alpine, where you can count on one hand the cars you pass. Fortunately, the physical isolation of Big Bend National Park from the rest of Texas and the United States makes it one of the best destinations for genuine wilderness adventure and exploration.

Driving south from Marathon, US 385 crosses the Chihuahuan desert's rolling countryside, where antelope graze in the tall grasses and hawks and vultures circle overhead. The road follows the old Comanche War Trail, the route to Mexico that the Comanche tribes followed each September during their annual raiding parties. The raids, which began in the 1700s, ceased over a hundred years later when the U.S. Army established a string of cavalry forts to protect the settlers.

Chisos Basin

Most visitors begin their journey through Big Bend National Park in the Chisos Basin, the most frequented area in the park. The basin, a valley surrounded by the tall Chisos Mountains, lies at 5,500 feet elevation. Throughout the year the basin is considerably cooler than the surrounding desert and offers easy access to many mountain hiking trails. The Chisos Mountains, including the tallest peak in the Chisos area, Mount Emory at 7,835 feet, tower thousands of feet above the lodge, campgrounds, horse stables, and the basin's visitors center.

Hiking

Thirty-six hiking trails crisscross the park. The Panther Path, Window Trail, and six other self-guided trails (pamphlets are available at each trailhead) describe the geology and wildlife of the desert and mountains. The best guides are for the Panther Path, Lost Mine Trail, and Santa Elena Canyon Trail. A number of other primitive trails, not regularly maintained by the Park Service, are recommended only for experienced hikers in good physical condition.

If you plan on any extensive hiking in Big Bend National Park, pick up a map of the hiking trials from the Panther Junction visitors center. The sun is very hot during the summer (usually over 100° F), the trails are steep, and the altitude is above 5,000 feet. Carry at least a gallon of water per person a day, and on a hot day, more.

Horseback Riding and River Rafting

Chisos Remuda Saddle Horses, a licensed park concessionaire, leads horseback trail rides into the interior of the park. The rides start from the corrals, located down the hill from the Chisos Basin visitors center. The rides can be expensive—$45 for a day-long ride on the South Rim Trail.

Outfitting companies in the nearby towns Terlingua and Lajitas lead guided one- to five-day raft and canoe trips down the Rio Grande, on stretches of the river both inside and outside national-park boundaries. Trips lasting up to three weeks go down the Rio Grande Wild and Scenic River, beyond the park boundaries, and into the river's grueling lower canyons.

Experienced river runners can rent rafts and canoes for runs through Colorado, Santa Elena, Mariscal, and Bouquillas Canyons. The Big Bend Shuttle Service provides transportation to put-in and take-out spots, and the ranger station issues rafting permits. The best time of year for running the river is from September through November, right after the rainy season in the Mexican mountains.

Scenic Drives

Several scenic drives on paved roads through the park are well worth the time, weaving through eroded mesas, across ancient floodplains, and past exposed lava flows and compressed volcanic ash. You'll notice that the dry, clear air makes mountain ranges over fifty miles away look much, much closer. The forty-mile drive from Persimmon Gap at the park's north entrance to the Chisos Basin rises from Chihuahuan desert vegetation at 2,000 feet to pine forests at over 5,000 feet. A second, forty-seven-mile drive goes from the Chisos Basin to the Santa Elena Canyon Overlook. A third, sixty-three-mile drive goes from the overlook to the Rio Grande Village visitors center, at the far eastern border.

Another network of unimproved dirt roads leads to and ends at a number of remote campgrounds in the backcountry. A four-wheel-drive with high clearance is a must for most unimproved dirt roads. For a short off-road drive, try the interpretive auto trail to Dagger Flats. Or, if you have more time and extra water, pick up the dirt road near the base of Cerro Castellan and follow it as it parallels the Rio Grande and turns inland to Glenn

Spring. This is the most remote area of the park with the best examples of Chihuahuan desert flora.

Wildlife

Big Bend is rich in wildlife, most of which is plentiful and easily seen. Deer are common, javelinas and foxes openly roam the populated Chisos Basin, beavers live in reed lodges along the river, and eighteen species of bats have been seen in the park. The river canyons are closed to raft trips each spring, when endangered peregrine falcons nest in aeries along the canyon walls. Black bears and gray wolves still live in the Chisos Mountains.

Mountain lions also live in the Chisos, but are reclusive and rarely seen, except during drought periods when food and water supplies are low and the lions range into inhabited areas. If you should be lucky enough to see one and the lion doesn't retreat, stand still, wave your arms, and shout, and if that doesn't work, throw stones. Never run away or try to hide, actions that suggest you are some form of prey.

Four varieties of rattlesnakes live in the park, including the poisonous Trans-Pecos copperhead, usually seen in bamboo thickets along the river banks. You may see tarantulas, which are very common in the park but not poisonous, walking across the roads in the evening. Centipedes and scorpions are also fairly common inhabitants.

Plant Life

The Chihuahuan desert supports a unique set of plants, including the lechuguilla, an indicator plant for the Chihuahuan desert, found nowhere else. Other common plants include the barrel

This Trans-Pecos snake is a handsome yellow and black

cactus, ocotillo, prickly pear, cholla, and peyote. At higher elevations, where the Chihuahuan desert gives way to forest, you'll find three types of juniper, Douglas fir, ponderosa pine, and oak.

Where: Follow US 385 south from Marathon, or US 118 from Alpine, to the National Park. If you are coming from Presidio, take FM 170 east to Study Butte.
Hours: The park is open year-round.

Admission: Pay a nominal admission fee by stopping at the Panther Junction visitors center on your way into the park.

Best time to visit: February to May and September to November. The climate in the Chisos Basin is comfortable year-round.

Activities: Rafting, canoeing, camping, backpacking, hiking, horseback riding, wildlife observation, scenic drives, and fishing.

Concessions: Chisos Mountains Lodge, in the Chisos Basin, has thirty-four rooms. A restaurant in the Chisos Basin is open daily, but if you plan on eating there, check its open hours. Gift shops are located at Panther Junction, in Rio Grande Village, and in the Chisos Basin. Chisos Remuda Saddle Horses conducts half- and full-day horseback rides in the park. If you plan a raft trip on the Rio Grande, reconfirm your dates to check water levels before leaving home.

Pets: Not allowed on any trails or in the backcountry.

Other: Watch for poisonous snakes and be prepared to seek immediate help. The park also has poisonous giant centipedes and poisonous scorpions, neither of which are considered lethal. Books, available from the Panther Junction visitors center, describe the geology and vegetation you'll see along the roadways.

For more information:

Superintendent, Big Bend National Park, TX 79834; 915-477-2236.

Big Bend Shuttle Service, 915-371-2523.

BIG BEND RANCH STATE NATURAL AREA

It is unfortunate that Texas's largest state park, at 265,000 acres, also happens to be the most remote. The only road access into

Desert tarantulas can measure four inches from leg tip to leg tip

Big Bend Ranch State Natural Area is along FM 170, between Lajitas and Presidio. Most of the interior is currently inaccessible, with only one road branching off FM 170 heading into the backcountry. In addition, only two hiking trails, totaling thirty miles, have been built and are maintained. The area's unique attractions make it worth the effort: some of the tallest waterfalls in the state, rafting on the Rio Grande, extremely tough road and mountain biking, long hiking trails, and ancient Native American sites.

Established in 1989, the Big Bend Ranch State Natural Area is only just beginning to develop visitors facilities. Access is limited to foot trails and the Solitario Overlook access road. Campsites along the river are primitive, with no electricity or facilities. The state of Texas is still attempting to acquire tracts of private land in the area and has yet to finalize plans to improve the park's recreational facilities. If you like wild and unspoiled areas, visit now before the park's inevitable popularity brings in large crowds.

Park Tours

The easiest and best way to see the backcountry is by bus. Guided tours organized out of the Barton Warnock Environmental Center in Lajitas drive up the river on FM 170 and turn inland for thirty miles to the Solitario/Fresno Overlook. The tour guides thoroughly explain the ecology and geology of the Big Bend region and point out items of interest. Lunch is included in the tour fee. The Barton Warnock Environmental Education Center, west of Big Bend National Park, functions as park headquarters. You can't miss the center—it is one of the very few buildings along the roadway.

Scenic Drives

If you are driving your own car to the Solitario Overlook, stop by the Warnock Center first for a map of the area and to check the weather forecast. The road west is steep and frequently washed out by flash floods during the rainy season. You will see more by stopping along the way at the frequent pullouts and campgrounds. Binoculars, sturdy hiking boots, a bottle of water, and a hat will make your drive up the river and walks in the park's mountains more rewarding.

One of the park's most fascinating areas, the Solitario Depression, lies deep in the heart of the wilderness area, along the park's only mountain road. The turnoff onto the road that leads to the Solitario Overlook is located on the western edge of the state natural area, about four miles east of Fort Leaton State Historic Site and about seven miles east of Presidio. The overlook area, about a forty-five-minute drive into the park, offers a panoramic view of this geologic wonder. The depression was created over 500 million years ago when magma from the center of the earth, forcing its way up through the limestone crust, formed a depression of concentric rings five miles in diameter. In the distance you can see the gashes in the earth that make up Fresno Canyon.

In Fresno Canyon, south of the Solitario Depression, are the state's second and third highest waterfalls, Mexicano Falls and Madrid Falls, both over 100 feet high. Water plunges over steep cliffs, creating oases of green in the arid hills. Fresno Canyon lies in the heart of the Bofecillos Mountains, which rise to over 5,000 feet above sea level. Dozens of remote, rarely visited caves are decorated with Indian pictographs dating from 3,000 B.C.

Recreation

The most rigorous activity in the park is bicycling up and down the steep hills on the road from Lajitas to Presidio. Only for cyclers in top condition, this ride will quickly exhaust even the best riders. Carry lots of water, and a pace car is a good idea.

Hiking and backpacking are popular along the park's trails, but also require a hefty dose of stamina and strength, especially during the hot months from May to September. Carry at least one and a half gallons of water per person and leave the trailhead before the sun rises. A map and guidebook are available from the Warnock Center. A compass can be a lifesaver as well, but you need to know how to use it. This park is still very new, primitive, and undeveloped, although plans are in the works to build new trails into this wilderness.

River Rafting

The Texas Parks and Wildlife Department allows access for rafting to the Rio Grande at three points: Rancherias Canyon, Madera (Monilla) Canyon, and Grassy Banks. One-day float trips are popular through Colorado Canyon, with a put-in at Rancherias Canyon and take-out at Lajitas. Call the Warnock Center for information on arranging guided commercial or individual trips. The Big Bend Shuttle Service can assist you with the logistics of put-ins and take-outs.

Visitor Programs

Educational programs put on at the Warnock Center are outstanding. Children love the self-guided botanical gardens and interpretive exhibits on the region's history and environment. A special display narrates the destruction of grasslands through ranching and describes recent efforts to restore the region to its natural beauty.

Where: Barton Warnock Environmental Education Center is in Lajitas, on FM 170 east of town. Big Bend Ranch State Natural Area is located between Lajitas and Presidio. A patchwork of private tracts of land within the park boundaries is in the process of being acquired by the state.

Hours: Access to the state natural area is twenty-four hours a day year-round.

Admission: Bus tours in the state natural area cost $30. Nominal fee for camping and hiking on the trails.

Best time to visit: October through March. Summer can be brutally hot. The highest average daily temperatures in Texas are recorded near here, in Presidio, at 103°F in June, 102°F in July, and 100°F in August. The second all-time highest temperature in Texas, at 117°F, was also recorded in Presidio.

Activities: Hiking, camping, interpretive bus tours, biking, and river rafting.

Concessions: None.

Pets: Must be kept on a leash at all times.

Other: The road to the Solitario Depression is 160 miles round-trip from civilization. Carry extra water, supplies, and maintenance tools. The roads are very long, steep, and isolated.

For more information:

Big Bend Ranch State Natural Area and Barton Warnock Environmental Education Center, HCR 70, Box 375, Terlingua, TX 79853; 915-424-3327.

Fort Leaton State Historical Park, P.O. Box 1220, Presidio, TX 79845; 915-229-3613.

GUADALUPE MOUNTAINS NATIONAL PARK

The highest mountains in Texas, the Guadalupes, rise between El Paso and Carlsbad Caverns, New Mexico. The 86,416-acre Guadalupe Mountains National Park, established in 1966, is nestled in the heart of this quiet, pristine western corner of the state. Most visitors to this part of the country dip south to Big Bend National Park or head north over the New Mexico border to Carlsbad Caverns. Few stop at this national park, even though the mountains on the northern horizon, eighty miles away, are clearly visible.

The Mescalero Apaches believed that Guadalupe Peak, at 8,751 feet the highest peak in Texas, was home to their sacred fire god. Later, from 1860 to 1880, the Guadalupes were the site of a series of bloody Indian–U.S. Cavalry battles and the place where the Mescalero Apaches made their last stand before being driven from Texas.

Visitors Centers and Facilities

As the park is both young and remote, visitors facilities are rustic. This is a true outdoor traveler's destination. Other than the visitors centers, where there are rest rooms and drinking water, facilities are few and far between. The nearest lodging is over thirty miles away, and there are no gas stations or food stores, so bring what you need. If you are looking for a wilderness experience, the Guadalupe Mountains are it.

There are two visitors centers in the park. The Frijole visitors center and park headquarters are located east of Guadalupe Pass near the Frijole Ranch. The McKittrick visitors center, only a few miles from the New Mexico border, is in the northeast corner of the park.

Most visitors who enter the park choose to first stop at the McKittrick visitors center, and then hike into McKittrick Canyon, considered by many the most scenic mountain canyon in Texas. The campgrounds near the Frijole visitors center are never filled.

Hiking

Whether you car-camp or backpack, the only way to see the park is on the hiking trails. Elevation gains of up to 3,000 feet make some of the trails very strenuous, while others have little elevation gain and are rated easy to moderate. Because of the park's high elevation, the sun is deceptively strong and the nights sometimes surprisingly cold.

Visitors will tell you the best hiking in the park is in McKittrick Canyon, a wooded area with several species of pine trees, junipers, and walnuts. Before heading into the backcountry, get to know some of these trees by first walking the 0.8-mile interpretive trail near the visitors center. The rangers can tell you about the weather and recent animal sighting in the canyon. The canyon trail probably gives you the best opportunities for seeing the spectacular vistas of the Guadalupe Mountains. The Permian Reef Geologic Trail has many marine fossils in the mountain walls along the paths. The reef system that forms these mountains is the largest known exposed mountain reef system recorded in the United States.

Any reasonably ambitious hiker should try the 8.8-mile round-trip hike from Pine Springs Campground to the top of Guadalupe Peak. The elevation gain makes this a moderately difficult hike, but well worth the effort. Panoramic views from the trail of Shumard Peak, El Capitan, Hunter Peak, and Lost Peak are awesome. Besides the strenuous El Capitan Trail, to the top of El Capitan, you can choose from a number of easier trails. Devil's Hall Trail and the trail to Hunter Peak are somewhat easier going and offer rewarding exposures of ancient reef limestone and deep lush canyons.

Camping and Backpacking

Two drive-in campsites, the favored being Pine Springs, are located near park headquarters. However, in the summer, if you have the time, plan on overnighting at Dog Canyon Campground, where at 6,300 feet elevation, temperatures are cooler and more pleasant. However, the only access to Dog Canyon is through New Mexico, and for Texans this often means several extra hours of driving.

Many outdoor adventurers opt for backpack camping.

Twelve hiking trails loop and circle through the park, leading to nine separate established backcountry campsites. More than eighty miles of hiking trails are maintained in the park. Extended treks are a favorite of regulars, but you must bring water (don't count on finding any potable water once you're on the trail), food, and a topographic map.

For people who enjoy snow camping, the beautiful snow-bound Guadalupes are a good destination in winter. Temperatures can be quite cold and the humidity low, but high winds whip the peaks, so pack carefully.

Horseback Riding

Over 80 percent of the park's trails are open to horseback riding. With two corrals available for public use, it is very common to see visitors on horseback in the backcountry. Some trails are closed during heavy rainstorms. Ask for a copy of the horseback trail guide at the ranger station, which rates the difficulty and conditions of various trails. The Park Service discourages inexperienced riders due to the exposure and altitude of most trails.

Wildlife

Expect to see a fair amount of true wildlife throughout the park, animals mostly not accustomed to encounters with man, including panthers, white-tailed deer, coyotes, bears, elk, and bobcats. If you have the opportunity, night hikes can be a special experience, as you might catch a glimpse of the park's nocturnal animals, including porcupines, ringtails, and bobcats. Be careful, though; the rangers aren't excited about rescuing people who fall into canyons in the dark. Ask for a bird checklist at the visitors center, which lists approximately 290 bird species frequenting these mountains. While most amateur bird-watchers were on the lookout for the park's numerous raptor species, we preferred the plentiful and colorful passerines and hummingbirds.

Where: Follow State 54 north from Van Horn and I-10, and merge with US 62 on the outskirts of the national park. If coming from El Paso, take US 62 east until it begins to wind its way up to the entrance to the park.

Hours: Open daily year-round.

Admission: Nominal entrance fee. No fee for backcountry camping permits.

Best time to visit: March to June and September to November. Carry cold-weather gear during the fall and spring, when temperatures can drop and rise over 40°F in just a few hours. During the cold months from autumn to spring be sure to take a high-quality windbreaker, as winds exceeding sixty miles per hour are not uncommon and can quickly lead to hypothermia.

Activities: Hiking, backpacking, camping, wildlife observation, and bird-watching.

Concessions: There are no stores or gas stations in the park. Corrals are provided for horses. The nearest store is over thirty miles away.

Pets: Not allowed outside the parking lot and camping areas.

For more information:

Guadalupe Mountains National Park, HC 60, Box 400, Salt Flat, TX 79847; 915-828-3251.

DAVIS MOUNTAINS REGION

The Davis Mountains, the second highest mountain range in Texas, lie between Big Bend and the Guadalupe Mountains, south of I-10 and northwest of Fort Davis. Mount Livermore, the second highest peak in Texas, rises to 8,206 feet above sea level and is snowcapped in the winter. At an average elevation of one mile above sea level and with mild summers and chilly winters, the Davis Mountains area is a favorite destination for Texans from the Hill Country, Houston, and the Dallas–Fort Worth area. Its gold mine of outdoor recreation alternatives, combined with temperate weather, has greatly increased the region's popularity in recent years.

Davis Mountains State Park

At an elevation of over 5,000 feet, 1,320-acre Davis Mountains State Park is one of the most popular camping areas in these high rolling hills. The park superintendent recommends making reservations for the campgrounds during spring, summer, and fall weekends. In addition to the seasonal Limpia Creek, and a number of hiking trails and streamside campsites, the area boasts its own herd of longhorn cattle.

Stop at the entrance station for schedules of local activities and information about the region's natural history. Naturalist slide shows are held in the amphitheater in the evening, a short walk from park headquarters. A scenic drive leads to two overlook points, with panoramic views of the Davis Mountains and Mount Livermore.

While in the park look for the Montezuma quail, Inca dove, yellow-bellied sapsucker, kestrel, and golden eagle, a few of the 184 bird species often seen in the area. Mammals include squirrels, raccoons, deer, coyotes, and bobcats. A visit to the mountains during spring is rewarded with wildflowers blooming red, blue, and yellow on the green, grassy hillsides.

Where: Located four miles north of Fort Davis on State 118, along the road to McDonald Observatory.
Hours: Open year-round.

Admission: Nominal entrance and campsite fee.
Best time to visit: April through November, though summer can at times be hot. Winter brings cooler weather and snowstorms.
Activities: Hiking, camping, picnicking, scenic drives, wildlife viewing, and bird-watching.
Pets: Allowed only on a leash.
For more information:

Davis Mountains State Park, Box 786, Fort Davis, TX 79734; 915-426-3337.

Chihuahuan Desert Research Institute

Southeast of Davis Mountains State Park is the 580-acre Chihuahuan Desert Research Institute, founded by Sul Ross University, for the study of the ecology of the Chihuahuan desert. Open to the public daily during the summer, the research institute is an excellent place for children to discover the flora and fauna of the Chihuahuan desert.

The institute offers for sale a wide variety of desert plants to help support its environmental research activities. Educational programs for amateur ecologists interested in desert wildlife are offered on request. Visit the arboretum and learn about the differences among cacti, ocotillo, and yucca. Stroll the nature trails, and in a short time you'll know more about desert habitats than most local Texans. The Chihuahuan Desert Research Institute is a good place to start your education in West Texas's environment, especially if this is your first visit to the region.

Where: South of Fort Davis on US 118, on the road to Alpine. Follow the signs to the research center.
Hours: Open 9:00 A.M. to 5:00 P.M. on weekends, and weekday afternoons.

Admission: No fee.
Best time to visit: September through May.
Activities: Nature trails, educational programs.
Concessions: The institute sells cacti and other plants native to the Chihuahuan desert to support its research on rangeland ecology.
Other: Call ahead to make sure the trails and arboretum are open, since times change throughout the year.
For more information:
    Chihuahuan Desert Research Center, 915-837-8370.

McDonald Observatory

Thirteen miles north of Davis Mountains State Park, at the top of Mount Locke, at 6,800 feet, is McDonald Observatory, where the world's largest telescope open for pubic viewing is on display. However, because the observatory is a scientific research center, a full docket of experiments keeps the telescope busy around the clock and limits public access. In the same facility are several other telescopes and equipment for picking up radio waves and millimeter waves from deep-sky objects. The altitude and distance from city lights make this one of the best locations in the United States for viewing the skies.

A well-maintained exhibit of photos and astronomical research at the visitors information center gives you your first peek into the observatory's scientific research program. Tours of the large white dome that covers the telescope are conducted in late afternoon during summer.

Amateur astronomers hold star parties in the lower parking area on Tuesday, Friday, and Saturday nights. You don't need your own personal telescope to view the star-filled sky, since many amateur astronomers from as far away as Houston bring their six- to eighteen-inch telescopes, set them up, and invite curious beginners to take their first up-close view of the heavens. Dozens of people wait in line to look through the eyepieces pointing at the night skies. Popular celestial sights include planets, galaxies, nebulae, and globular clusters. Once started, these "parties" go on into the wee hours of the morning.

Where: Thirteen miles north from Davis Mountains State Park on US 118.

Hours: The 107-inch telescope is open only one day a month for public viewing, so call for the day and hours. During the summer months, the dome is open daily for tours. The W. L. Moody, Jr., visitors information center is open daily except holidays. Star parties gather at the visitors center on Tuesday, Friday, and Saturday nights from 6:30 P.M. until 1:00 to 3:00 A.M.

Admission: No fee.

Best time to visit: Anytime during the year, though winter can be cold, blustery, and snowy.

Activities: Astronomy.

Concessions: A well-stocked gift shop at the visitors information center sells books and star charts.

For more information:

McDonald Observatory, P.O. Box 1337, Fort Davis, TX 79734; 915-426-3640.

Fort Davis National Historic Site

Down the hill from Davis Mountains State Park is Fort Davis National Historic Site. Operated by the National Park Service, it is one of the best-preserved examples of an 1800s cavalry fort. Once the home and headquarters of the renowned Buffalo Soldiers of the Indian wars (the 9th U.S. Cavalry), the fort was established in 1854 to protect travelers and settlers from Comanche and Apache raids. Later, during the Civil War, the fort was abandoned by the 9th Cavalry and eventually was burned to the ground by the Mescalero Apaches. After the Civil War the Buffalo Soldiers went on the offensive against the Apaches, and reconstruction of the fort began. Soon after the building was complete, the Apaches were defeated. By 1891, Fort Davis was again deserted. In 1961 the National Park Service designated the site a national historic site.

Three hiking paths loop through in the park. If you are camping at the state park, you can drive to the fort or hike the 4.5-mile North Ridge Trail that links the park to the fort. The second longest trail, at three miles, is the Hospital Trail, which starts behind the old hospital and loops around to the north back to Officers' Row, a series of restored cavalry officer quarters. The Tall Grass Nature Trail leads to an overlook on the hills above the fort.

Where: From Fort Stockton, follow US 118 north toward Davis State Park. The national historical site is on the outskirts of town.

Hours: Open daily year-round. Closed on holidays. During summer the park staff wears period dress and uniforms.

Best time to visit: May through November. Winter can be windy and chilly.

For more information:

Fort Davis National Historic Site, P.O. Box 1456, Fort Davis, TX 79734; 915-426-3224.

HUECO TANKS STATE HISTORICAL PARK

Hanging by her fingertips from the drop-off, she twists her body, catlike, until her foot finds a small crevice in the rock. To prevent a fatal fall, the blue-green climbing rope attached to her safety harness loops through several carabiners (fasteners) placed at fifteen-foot intervals up the cliff. Reaching into a bag of chalk at her waist, the climber dusts her sweaty hands and in a few more deft moves disappears over the top of the cliff.

She and many other rock climbers consider the 860-acre Hueco Tanks State Historical Park, thirty-two miles east of El Paso, the second best place to rock-climb in Texas after Enchanted Rock. Anthropologists, geologists, naturalists, and history buffs also come to Hueco Tanks to study the unusual rock formations, visit the ruins of the Butterfield–Overland Mail Route station, see Indian pictographs, and discover the park's vernal pools.

The small park encircles three tall, massive rock formations, known as North, West, and East Mountains. There is a fair amount of disagreement about the origin of these massifs and the strange hollows and depressions (*huecos*) in the tops of the rocks that act as rainwater reservoirs. The mountains, bulging up out of the Chihuahuan desert, are the result of intrusive volcanic activity about thirty-four million years ago. This park has proven to be a popular destination for hiking, picnicking, rock climbing, and camping.

The three mountains are unique because of the numerous deep pits weathered into the tops of the rocks that form natural rainwater basins. Some of these are large, others quite small, but all are critically important to the ecosystem and to the survival of several kinds of freshwater crustaceans. Rainwater trapped in the huecos becomes the spawning ground for three species of shrimp that live out a complete life cycle in the huecos. During the dry summer season, the eggs dry out and become dormant, waiting for the next rain. When the rains finally come, the eggs hatch and grow to maturity, and new eggs are laid. The water and shrimp, near the bottom of the food chain, provide important sustenance to small animals and birds.

A bird checklist, available from park headquarters, lists over 200 species observed in the area. Vultures and hawks are regularly seen circling overhead; swifts, swallows, and bluebirds occupy the lower stories of the forest. Coyotes, deer, wild turkeys, and even mountain lions are occasional visitors to the preserve. Ringtails and bobcats hunt field mice in the park at night.

Long ago, the rock's natural reservoirs brought Kiowas, Apaches, and later, pioneers, to the park. Paleo-Indian stone

Mountain lions often hunt during the day for deer as well as mice, raccoons, and even grasshoppers

tools, arrowheads, and spearpoints recovered from the archaeo-logical sites date back to 8,000 B.C. Many of the over 5,000 rock paintings, located in twelve major groupings throughout the park, are the work of more contemporary tribes like the Mes-calero Apaches and Comanches. Pictographs from other older tribes date back to 2,000 B.C.

For a bit of recent history, make a quick visit to the aban-doned stagecoach station. Imagine horses and drivers rolling into the dusty, hot small town. In the mid-1800s the water at Hueco Tanks supported a small pioneer community and frontier outpost.

There are no established hiking trails in the park. You may hike and climb anywhere, with only two rules: don't touch, deface, or mar the pictographs, and don't disturb the fragile ecosystems in the huecos.

Where: Located thirty-two miles east of El Paso. Take US 62 (the same road that leads to the Guadalupe Mountains) east for twenty-six miles. Turn north onto Ranch Road 2775, which leads to the entrance.
Hours: Open daily.
Admission: Nominal entrance fee, additional fee for camping.
Best time to visit: March to May and September to November.
Activities: Camping, hiking, rock climbing, bird-watching, wildlife observation, picnicking, and studying the Indian picto-graphs and the vernal pools.
Concessions: None.
Pets: Must be kept on a leash.
Other: The park offers tours of the Indian pictographs during summer, from June to August. There are slide shows on the history and wildlife of Hueco Tanks in the evenings at the amphitheater.
For more information:
Hueco Tanks State Historical Park, Route 3, Box 1, El Paso, TX 79935; 915-857-1135.

MONAHANS SANDHILLS STATE PARK

Conjuring up visions of Lawrence of Arabia, miles and miles of tall, rolling sand dunes at Monahans Sandhills State Park bake under the scorching summer sun. Year after year the elements shape and reshape the dunes in the 3,840-acre park, just off I-20 between Midland and Odessa. Howling windstorms whip up vast quantities of fine sand, eroding and building the dunes, but never really moving them.

The park covers just over six square miles, a tiny portion of a larger sandy dune desert that stretches hundreds of miles northwest from here into New Mexico. Most of these dunes, however, are covered with vegetation and have ceased to grow and change.

The sand dunes at Monahans rise over seventy feet high behind the park entrance and visitors center. Remarkably, this nearly barren landscape was once the site of many Indian battles, one tribe against another. And for what?

Interpretive exhibits in the visitors center describe the unique ecology of this desert, which provides a habitat for several unusual plants and animals. Across these apparently unproductive dunes one of the largest single-species oak forests in the United States thrives. These trees, dwarf Havard shin oaks, only about four feet tall, provided acorns, an important source of food for the Apaches and Comanches. They also indicated the presence of a ground-water supply near the surface.

Today there are no more Indians, the Comanches and Apaches having been driven out in the late 1800s. Now, the Texas Parks and Wildlife Department manages a small corner of the dune field for the recreational use of the public. The park is open to exploration on foot. You'll feel lost in another world while wandering among the cactus, morning glories, and shin oaks in the deep valleys between the dunes.

Before climbing up the dunes, stop by the visitors center and read about the geology of the sand hills, their Indian history, and their subsequent discovery by the Spanish. Outside the center is a short interpretive trail that takes less than half an hour to walk and helps you identify local vegetation. Except for the short walk, there are no marked trails. You are free to wander all over the sand dunes and explore anywhere on foot. Later, out on the dunes, you'll be able to pick out the tracks of a sidewinder rattlesnake or a desert mouse, and to identify sagebrush, bindweed, and mesquite.

During the summer, the sand becomes a hotplate, driving wildlife to take refuge under the shrubs and even dig down into the sand. Summer visitors are rare to this American Sahara. The most appealing time of the year is during the rainy fall and spring. The cooling downpours and lower temperatures transform the apparent wasteland into a park full of wildlife and fun.

In fact, after a rainstorm small pools of water form at the lowest points among the dunes, attesting to the abundance of water just inches under the surface of the sand. These pools attract animals and, if you're patient, provide one of the best ways to see wildlife in the sandy wastes. In the evening, jackrabbits, foxes, and coyotes share the vital water. In the morning, tracks in the sand attest to the drama of life in the dunes, until the wind erases the evidence of the night's hunt.

After spending a few hours wandering the dunes, borrow a plastic disc from park headquarters, find the pinnacle of the dunes, and slide to the bottom. It is an exhilarating way to end a visit to this state park.

Where: Five miles east of Monahans and south of I-20. From Odessa, travel thirty miles west on I-20 and pick up Park Road 41 to the park's entrance.
Hours: Open daily.
Admission: Nominal entrance fee, additional fee for camping.
Best time to visit: October through May. There are few visitors in the summer, the hottest time of year.
Activities: Wildlife observation, hiking the dunes, camping, and playing on the sand.

Concessions: None.

Pets: Must be kept on a leash.

For more information:

Monahans Sandhills State Park, Box 1738, Monahans, TX 79756; 915-943-2092.

ODESSA METEOR CRATER

Some 20,000 years ago, long before man inhabited this area, the earth passed through what is thought to have been the residue of a comet's tail. Thousands of nickel-iron meteorites broken off the comet by the earth's and sun's gravity plunged through the atmosphere at thousands of miles per hour, glowing white hot and visible for hundreds of miles. While most smaller meteorites vaporized, the larger ones didn't, and they slammed into the earth.

The largest of the meteors, estimated to be around 1,000 tons, plunged through the atmosphere and smashed into the ground with the force of a nuclear weapon, excavating an impact crater over 500 feet across. Today we call this ancient hole in the ground the Odessa Meteor Crater. Nearby, dozens of smaller craters speckle the earth, probably formed from pieces broken off when the main asteroid entered the earth's atmosphere.

In subsequent centuries, blowing dust and sandstorms filled most of the crater and obliterated the many smaller, shallower craters sprinkled nearby. Pieces of small meteorites are still being unearthed across hundreds of square miles around the crater, and are finding their way into local curio shops.

Astronomers and scientists have dug exploratory trenches into the crater to learn more about meteorites and the physics of a large astral body entering the atmosphere and creating such an immense impact crater. The research is important to scientists who believe that the extinction of the dinosaurs was caused by a similar, but much older and larger, meteor strike.

Odessa, the second largest meteor crater in the United States and sixth largest in the world, is a reminder that the solar system can be a violent, unforgiving place.

Where: Located 5.5 miles west of Odessa.
Hours: Open daily.
Admission: No fee.

SEMINOLE CANYON STATE HISTORICAL PARK

Seminole Canyon State Historical Park, forty-five miles west of Del Rio on the Rio Grande, has one of the most impressive displays of Indian pictographs in Texas, some dating back 8,000 years. The 2,173-acre park, named after the Seminole Indians, the last Indians to occupy this area of Texas and Mexico, contains artifacts dating from up to 12,000 years ago. Stone tools and woven mats have been recovered from home sites built into caves along the cliffs of the Rio Grande. Vast caves and overhangs, the result of unusual weathering and erosion, made this stretch along the river a suitable place for nomadic tribes to settle.

Unfortunately, the Amistad Reservoir dammed up seventy-four miles of the Rio Grande, inundating many of these ancient Indian sites. Fortunately, though, three of the best examples of ancient Indian life have been preserved. The three sites—Fate Bell Shelter, Panther Cave, and Parida Cave—can be visited only by boat on the Rio Grande, or on foot accompanied by a ranger. Check at the ranger station for the schedule of guided tours. Of the three sites, Fate Bell is easiest to get to, a short walk below the visitors center along the Canyon Trail. The floor of the cave has thirteen feet of packed debris holding the secrets of 6,000 years of habitation. Rock paintings cover the walls.

To visit Panther and Parida Caves, you need to arrange for a boat tour. Parida Cave is impressive for its hundreds of pictographs, but Panther Cave contains benchmark pictographs against which all other West Texas pictographs are dated and measured. The paintings cover the sides and roof of the cave.

Even if Indian history doesn't pique your interest, the park is still worth a visit. In the effort to preserve some very fine ancient Indian pictographs and homesites, the state also created a quiet nature preserve along the banks of the Rio Grande. The water and riparian forest support a large population of ringtails, badgers, coyotes, and javelinas. In the evening, hikers enjoy the six-mile round-trip Rio Grande Trail that runs along the rim of the cliffs to the overlook above the water. Bring along your binoculars and a flashlight and plan to watch the sun set over the water.

If you're quiet, you'll be rewarded with ample opportunities to glimpse park animals. Bats swirl and swoop, silhouetted against the evening sky as they echo-locate and hunt insects. Coyotes and foxes can be seen edging down to the water at dusk.

Below and around you, notice how the three vegetation zones merge in the Seminole Canyon area, supporting a variety of animal life. South Texas thornbush mesquite merges with Chihuahuan Desert cacti and Edward's Plateau oaks. If you happen across this corner of Texas on your travels, stop and take a look. It's well worth the time.

Where: About forty-five miles west of Del Rio on US 90. Follow the signs to the park entrance.
Hours: Open daily.
Admission: Nominal entrance fee, additional fee for camping.
Best time to visit: October to April. This park lies on the eastern fringes of the Chihuahuan desert, and temperatures in the summer can be oppressive, reaching over 100°F.
Activities: Hiking, wildlife observation, boating to the Indian pictograph sites, picnicking, and camping. Backpacking on the Rio Grande Hiking Trail is not permitted.

Concessions: None.

Pets: Allowed only on a leash.

For more information:

Seminole Canyon State Historical Park, Box 820, Comstock, TX 78837; 915-292-4464.

3

Southeast Texas

INTRODUCTION

The Piney Woods, Texas's most diverse but least frequently visited wilderness area, located in the state's southeastern corner, is a heavily forested region of mixed national preserve, national forest, state park, and private land. The area ranges from the Gulf of Mexico northward to around Nacogdoches, and from the Houston area east to the Louisiana border.

Although the original old-growth forest covered about 3.5 million acres, human habitation and exploitation have cut it to only 300,000 acres of wooded forest and swamps, less than one-tenth of its original size.

The history of the Big Thicket region is a story of the exploitation of natural resources: tree farming, oil exploration, and population expansion. In the early 1800s, commercial loggers began harvesting both hardwood and pine. After the Civil War, population growth led to further deforestation. Oil exploration began around the turn of the century, bringing in roads and boomtowns.

Today tree farming still mutilates the forest. The last bear roamed the forest decades ago. Whole tracts of forest have been cleared, the scars visible from the roadways. At the Woodville depot, in the geographic center of the Big Thicket, felled trees stacked four stories high tower over the roadway. The destruction of the forest finally slowed in 1974 with the creation of the Big Thicket National Preserve, but logging continues in Sam Houston, Angelina, Davy Crockett, and Sabine National Forests, which together total about 661,000 acres.

Despite this significant habitat loss, the Big Thicket region still offers outdoor adventurers a world of forests, rivers, and lakes. On the region's lakes and rivers, canoeing and motorboating provide access to a snarl of rarely explored backwaters. Botanists and ornithologists join weekenders on hikes in the forest, and equestrian buffs saddle up for trail rides through the woods. Bicyclers and backpackers vanish into the farthest points of the forest.

The parks, preserves, and sanctuaries that protect what remains of this once grand and stately forest draw visitors back time and again. If you plan to visit, come between September and June. The summer months are oppressively hot and humid.

The defining characteristic of the Big Thicket is the intermingling of eight different forest and vegetation zones. Wetland and dryland savannas, sandylands, palmetto-oak forests, floodplains, pine uplands, mixed-hardwood and pine-slope forests, and baygall swamps all meet in a collage that biologists say makes this region one of the most diverse ecosystems in the United States.

Approximately 300 bird, 1,000 wildflower, and 150 tree and bush species are found here, as well as many mammals and reptiles. This diversity earned worldwide recognition in 1981, when the United Nations added the 86,000-acre Big Thicket National Preserve to its list of International Biosphere Reserves, one of only 250 regions so honored.

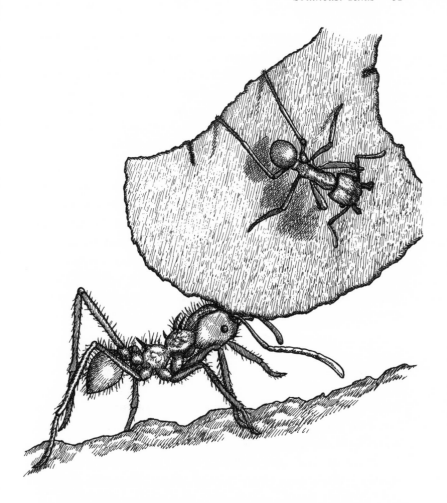

Leaf-cutter ants cut and carry leaves, fruit, flowers, and grass

Evidence of the diversity are cacti that grow on arid sandy-lands not more than a dozen feet from swamplands hosting water lilies and carnivorous floating plants. Winding, twisting water-ways, wetland savannas, and dry savannas provide ideal habi-tats for songbirds, raptors, and carrion birds. Once-endangered American alligators glide through the bayous while snakes slither through the canebrake (native American bamboo). Birds flit from tree to tree under the forest canopy.

Sometimes the Big Thicket seems almost out of place in Texas, the proverbial cowboy country.

BIG THICKET NATIONAL PRESERVE

In 1974, the U.S. Department of the Interior set aside 85,736 acres of original pine forest in East Texas as the Big Thicket National Preserve, an area divided into eight land units and four waterway corridor units. The twelve units, intermixed with private land, lie within an area stretching from Beaumont north to Lake B. A. Steinhagen and from the Neches River west to the Trinity River. Present plans for the preserve include the acquisition and inclusion of an additional 10,000 to 15,000 acres.

Recreation

Outdoor recreation in the preserve is almost limitless. Established trails exist in most of the preserve's units, although bushwhacking is allowed anywhere within the preserve's boundaries. A number of short interpretive trails and trail guides are maintained by the National Park Service. Canoeists paddle through and fish in the labyrinthine bayous. Horseback riding is popular on the few trails where it is permitted. Without question the most exciting and popular activities are wildlife identification and bird-watching.

No developed campgrounds exist in the Big Thicket National Preserve, but primitive camping is allowed anywhere away from streams and structures. Pack in the water you'll need, since the water in the park is not drinkable.

Wildlife

Beaver, opossum, white-tailed deer, coyote, raccoon, bobcat, armadillo, and alligator all make their home in the preserve. Over 300 bird species, including raptors and vultures, swoop and soar through these forests. Over fifty kinds of reptiles have been identified, including cottonmouth water moccasins, coral snakes, and several species of pit vipers. Fire ants, wasps, and bees are common, and mosquitoes are ever-present.

In spring, usually from February through April, hundreds of types of flowering plants and trees turn the forest into a palette of pastels. Rattan and other climbing vines mix with over twenty fern species, lending the forest a jungle atmosphere. Eight plant species found in the Big Thicket represent four of the five carnivorous plant families found in the United States. There are seventeen species of native orchids.

Hiking and Canoeing

Before hiking or camping in the forest, stop at the Big Thicket visitors information station seven miles north of Kountze, on the southern edge of the Turkey Creek Unit. Park rangers can point out where to find elusive or rare plants and animals, and tell you how to avoid snakes and other hazards. Remember to carry your own water in the preserve. Creek and pond water is very acidic and not drinkable.

Well-maintained hiking trails cross through some of the preserve's units. To get a taste of this unusual area, you have to get out of your car and walk through the woods. Printed guides describing the habitat, plants, and wildlife are available at most trailheads.

Canoeing is also a good way to explore the corridor units,

on day outings through winding bayous or on overnight canoe-camping trips along the rivers, which are generally remote, quiet, and rarely visited. The national preserve's information station issues free backcountry permits for camping and provides information on canoe rentals and outfitters.

Educational Programs

The National Park Service conducts informational and interpretive programs, including guided hikes and river trips. One veteran visitor who regularly hikes in the Hickory Creek Savanna Unit suggested we join a ranger-guided tour for newcomers. It wasn't until the ranger showed us the small, reddish, insect-eating sundew, a carnivorous plant, that we could pick it out along the trail. The Park Service also conducts children's activities, such as "Kid's Wilderness Survival" and "Through the Looking Glass." Wildflower and carnivorous-plant "walk-and-talks," canoe tours, and night prowls through the forest are also offered, as are advanced workshops on birding, wildflower identification, canoeing, and backpacking.

Turkey Creek Unit

Turkey Creek, 7,800 acres, is the most interesting unit in the preserve and the easiest to reach. The park's information station, located at the south end of the unit, is near the trailheads for two interpretive hikes and the park's longest trail, a 17.5-mile hiking and backpacking path along Turkey Creek. At the north end of the unit is the entrance to the Pitcher Plant Trail, one of the most popular walks in the preserve.

A walk on the Kirby Nature Trail, with a short inner loop (1.7 miles) and a long outer loop (2.5 miles), gives you a good overview of several of the Big Thicket's different vegetation zones. The guide to this trail, available at both the trailhead and the information station, points out slope forests, towering tupelo and giant bald cypress trees, cypress knees emerging from the black baygall swamp, native American bamboo, and numerous flowering plants and trees.

The 17.5-mile Turkey Creek Trail, very long but flat, runs the length of the unit north and south, roughly paralleling the creek's flow. During rainy periods, parts of the trail may be flooded and impassable. Great backcountry camping sites are found all along this trail, which connects the Kirby Nature Trail in the south to the Pitcher Plant Trail in the north.

The Pitcher Plant Trail, a half mile of dirt path and wood boardwalk, winds through a classic example of mixed pine and beech forest and wetland savanna, a perfect habitat for orchids, pitcher plants, and sundews. In summer, the trail, which emerges from the forest and crosses open savannas, can be oven-hot. No drinking water is available once you enter the backcountry, so carry plenty with you. To get to the trailhead, which is wheelchair accessible, follow the signs off a well-maintained clay-dirt road running north-south from FM 1943 to FM 3063.

Hickory Creek Savanna Unit

The 668-acre Hickory Creek Savanna Unit, across State 69, is three miles north of the road leading to the Turkey Creek information station. One-half mile west off State 69, a dirt road leads south to the parking area for the Sundew Trail, named after the tiny carnivorous plant found in this forest.

This one-mile trail across raised wood boardwalks and dirt paths through wetland savanna and mixed forest is top-notch bird-watching territory. Open savannas offer excellent views of the forest canopy. Underneath, wildflowers and pitcher plants provide ground cover. To see the glistening red sundew plants, search in the flat grasses beside the trail where the outer loop trail splits away from the inner loop trail. The inner loop is wheel-chair accessible.

Big Sandy Creek Unit

This 14,300-acre unit encompasses a portion of Big Sandy Creek and stands of mature hardwood upland forests thick with beech, giant magnolia, pine, oak, and holly trees. This unit straddles FM 1276 and is bounded by the Alabama-Coushatta Indian Reservation on the north. Three hiking trails, including one that allows horseback riding, explore the area.

The Woodlands Trail, a 5.4-mile loop, begins in a planta-tion reforested in 1963 after loggers had cleared the area. You'll notice that the diameter of the trees is much smaller here than it is in the surrounding old-growth forest. The trail winds through pine and beech forests before dropping into the floodplain of Big Sandy Creek. Before hiking, check with the information station to see whether the trail is passable.

The 1.5-mile Beaver Slide Trail, the shortest trail in this unit, loops and winds alongside ponds and old beaver dams. This sandyland habitat supports thick forests of both pines and hard-woods. Rattan and other climbing vines hang in thick twists from the forest canopy. Notice that the forest floor has very little underbrush because of the sandy soil and lack of sunlight.

Big Sandy Creek Horse Trail, the only trail in the national preserve where you can ride horseback, passes through the unit's upland forests. Horseback riding is limited to day trips, and graz-ing on national-preserve property is not allowed. Introduction of hay into the preserve is forbidden in order to prevent the acci-dental introduction of non-native grasses. Rangers ask you to keep your horse on the trail and at least 100 feet from creeks and streams.

Beech Creek Unit

The well-marked entrance to the Beech Creek Unit's parking lot is located near the south edge of Lake B. A. Steinhagen, just off FM 2992, about four miles south of FM 1746.

The Beech Woods Trail, a one-mile path, is the best way to view the different growth stages of a sandyland forest. The trail begins in a mature stand of beech, magnolia, and loblolly trees. The thick forest canopy, over 100 feet above, causes the sandy floor to remain perpetually shaded, thus preventing the growth of wildflowers and low underbrush. Thick rattan vines loop and climb skyward, wrapping around beech trunks.

Farther along the trail, the forests are replaced by a tangle of briars and shrubs. According to the trail guide, the forests were devastated by the Southern pine beetle in the 1970s. Now the pines are just beginning to regrow. Other portions of the forest were heavily logged in the 1930s, and even now these areas are still recovering. Notice that the pines are sparse and much smaller in diameter than those in other parts of the preserve. Elsewhere, in the untouched portions of the forest, the forest floor is comparatively clear and tall trees grow in thick stands.

Over six miles of well-marked, unused dirt roads, which make for easy hiking, are quickly reverting to nature in this fertile forest.

Along the Neches River

The second longest length of protected river in the entire state, the Neches River runs for seventy-nine miles through remote, lush forest in five units of the national preserve, from Lake B. A. Steinhagen to the city of Beaumont. The river's central flow makes its way through a winding, twisting maze of swamplands, bayous, and creeks. With a good local map and some pioneer perseverance, you can find your way into any of the five units along the banks. But the easiest and most fascinating way to discover the preserve is by boat, preferably a canoe.

The five units—the Upper Neches River Corridor, Jack Gore Baygall Unit, Neches Bottom Unit, Lower Neches River Corridor, and Beaumont Unit—have a variety of waterways navigable by both novice and experienced boaters. The central river flow can be strong and swift, while backwater swamps, winding cypress sloughs, and bayou inlets are calm.

There are few improved public boat ramps along this stretch of river, but you can put in wherever roads cross the creek. To avoid getting lost in the myriad narrow channels and swampy bayous, pick up a topographic map from the Park Service and inquire about any recent changes in the river's course.

If you plan to camp out, pitch a tent on the sandbars in the river, not on the banks. Private property comes down to the shoreline in some places and owners have been known to evict trespassers. More important, though, the sandbars in the alluvial river are surprisingly free of mosquitoes and biting flies, which seem to swarm on the shoreline and in the forest. Slip into the river for relief from the heat and humidity, but watch out for alligators, a strong undertow, and submerged cypress roots, and afterward check for leeches.

If you want to canoe, call the preserve and ask for a "Canoe Trip Planner." This list of rivers, routes, and outfitters, with estimated costs for guides and canoe rentals, will be mailed to you without cost. Guided trips, both day and overnight, are given by the National Park Rangers along the Neches River and other, smaller creeks and streams in the preserve. If you choose the Neches, it is best to avoid the Lower Neches because of motorboat traffic out of Beaumont.

Along the river look for fine examples of baygall swamps wherever the channel widens into creeks and sloughs. The Jack

Gore Baygall Unit is the home of alligators and other swampland animals.

Along Little Pine Island Bayou

The two least-visited units are the Lance Rosier Unit and the Little Pine Island Bayou Corridor, which enclose twenty-five miles of the Little Pine Island Bayou between Saratoga and Beaumont. There are no improved hiking trails in either unit, only a network of dirt roads leading to ugly oil fields near Saratoga. You will find boat ramps where the bayou crosses State 69 on its way to meet the Neches River.

The Lance Rosier Unit encircles thick jungle-like hardwood-palmetto forests. Bald and tupelo cypress trees overgrown with Spanish moss grow in seasonally flooded, poorly drained flatlands. Oaks and other hardwoods that can tolerate flooded and saturated soil grow on either side of the bayou, and dwarf and Louisiana palms in the forest soar to more than twice their normal height.

Loblolly Unit

The 550-acre Loblolly Unit preserves a small but remarkable grove of loblolly pines and hardwoods north off State 105, between Batson and Moss Hill. This unit, the smallest in the preserve, was established to protect one of the very last stands of old-growth forest in Southeast Texas. Some of the trees are estimated to be over 150 years old. Unfortunately, the forest is full of feral pigs that have escaped from pig farmers in the area and thrive on plants and roots. If you walk in the forest, you're nearly certain to see some.

Where: Seven miles north of Kountze on US 69, look for the signs to the information station.

Hours: Open year-round, sunrise to sunset. Overnight campers must have a permit from the information station. The information station is closed on Christmas Day.

Admission: No fees for day visitors or overnight campers.

Best time to visit: February through May and September through December. In summer the weather is characterized by heavy rainfall, extreme humidity, and heat. With over fifty inches of annual rain, the Big Thicket is one of the wettest regions in Texas. Summer is oppressive with high temperatures between 90° and 100°F and humidity over 90 percent. In winter, the highs average in the 50s.

Activities: Camping, wildlife watching, bird-watching, hiking, horseback riding, biking, canoeing, boating, swimming, and interpretive programs. Contact the information station for scheduled educational programs.

Concessions: None. Food and gas are available in nearby Kountze and Woodville.

Pets: Not allowed in the backcountry. Horses are permitted only on select trails; contact the information station for locations.

Other: Many areas of the national preserve are prone to flooding. Hikers and boaters/canoeists can call the information station for the latest water levels. Mosquitoes, voracious year-round, can ruin an otherwise enjoyable trip; a DEET-based insect repellent is essential! Clothing impregnated with permethrin also provides good protection. If you see alligators on the banks or in the water, do *not* approach them, throw things, or taunt them. They seem docile and lethargic, but can move with lightning-fast aggressiveness when bothered by intruders. Venomous snakes, another hazard, are easy to avoid by watching where you step, not turning over logs, and not putting your foot or hand in unseen places.

For more information:

Superintendent, Big Thicket National Preserve, 3785 Milam, Beaumont, TX 77701; 409-839-2689.

For information on ranger programs, call the Big Thicket information station; 409-246-2337.

ROY E. LARSON SANDYLAND SANCTUARY

The Roy E. Larson Sandyland Sanctuary, located on 2,178 acres of sandyland habitat, encompasses eight miles of Village Creek, near where the creek crosses State 327, halfway between Silsbee and US 69. The Texas Nature Conservancy, a nonprofit conservation organization, manages the sanctuary.

This sanctuary, one of the few protected sandyland ecosystems in the Big Thicket, is a good example of the complex relationship of arid sandy soils and floodplain forests. The swamplands are in an advanced stage of ecological evolution as they move toward becoming wetland savannas. Farther from the river, baygall swamps and wetland savannas support a wide variety of birds and flowers. Tall pines throw deep shadows onto the forest floor.

Because visitors can hike, bird-watch, picnic, or canoe, this park is one of the most popular in the region. A large parking area, covered pavilion, picnic tables, and a grassy field make the sanctuary ideal for family outings.

Hiking

The three hiking trails in the park total 7.6 miles. On the 0.8-mile interpretive nature trail, a trail guide, available at the trailhead, describes fifteen posted stops in the forest of blackjack, bluejack, and red oak. Three types of pines live in East Texas. Longleaf and loblolly pine needles drift down to the forest floor. The third pine species, the shortleaf pine, is not native to the Big Thicket region, but was introduced by timber companies through reforestation programs. The Nature Conservancy is selectively burning the shortleaf pines to restore the natural ecology of the sanctuary.

A point of caution: The hiking trails in this section of forest are poorly marked, and it's easy to get lost. Watch for the white blazes at eye level on the trees. A guidebook and trail map are available at the trailhead and should be checked frequently.

Plants and Wildlife

In the spring, acres of wildflowers blanket the preserve. Wildflower buffs make a point of searching for rare orchids, but you don't have to be an aficionado to enjoy the colors. One of the most interesting flowers is the Carolina rockrose, a ten-inch-tall plant that flowers for only a few hours in spring. Carnivorous plants and water lilies float on the surface of the baygall swamps.

Between March and September you can see the flowers of the bull thistle, a plant specific to both sandylands and longleaf-pine uplands. Look for a splash of white star-shaped petals against a background of green stinging spines. The seeds are edible if you can get them without getting stung.

Visitors regularly report seeing coyotes, the largest carnivorous mammal in the Big Thicket, along hiking trails and in the forest. Bobcat prints cross the trail, evidence of last night's hunt for rabbits and squirrels, also common in the area. You may even spot the long, curving track of a snake. Unlike other forest habitats, the sandyland forests are relatively clear of shrubs and undergrowth, making them good for bird-watching. In the upper story of the forest songbirds can be heard and seen flying from tree to tree.

Not all anthills are the same, according to the trail guide, referring to a leaf-cutter ant colony a hundred yards down the path from the trailhead. The ants, which industriously cut sections of leaves and carry them back to the nest, form a strange parade of wriggling green leaves crossing the sandy white earth.

Canoeing

Canoeists will be happy to know that it's an easy paddle along the eight miles of Village Creek within the sanctuary. Before you go, however, you must arrange transportation back to your car after this one-way water adventure. On any given weekend, the slow-moving creek and quiet forest attract two or three canoeing parties.

Where: From Beaumont follow US 69 to Silsbee, then State 327 west to where the road crosses over Village Creek. The sanctuary is on the north side of the road.
Hours: Open daily, dawn to dusk. No overnight camping allowed.
Admission: No fee.
Best time to visit: February to May and September to December. Be prepared for rain anytime during the year.
Activities: Hiking, bird-watching, wildlife watching, and picnicking. Guided walks by the sanctuary management are available, but must be requested ahead of time. Canoeing is possible along Village Creek, from the intersection of FM 418 to the intersection of State 327.
Concessions: None.
Pets: Not allowed on the trails.
Other: You are still in the forests of the Big Thicket region, so be prepared for heat, humidity, and hungry mosquitoes and ticks. Locals tuck their pants into their socks to avoid ticks. Some trails are hard to follow, especially if you have a poor sense of

direction. The paths are often wet, so wear appropriate footwear.
For more information:

Roy E. Larson Sandyland Sanctuary, P.O. Box 909, Silsbee,
TX 77656; 713-385-4135.

ALABAMA-COUSHATTA INDIAN RESERVATION

Established in 1854, the Alabama-Coushatta Indian Reservation
is one of the few Indian reservations in the United States located
on heavily forested land. The home of the Alabama-Coushattas
encompasses 4,811 acres of piney woods and 26-acre Lake Tom-
bigbee. Hardly the largest preserve in the Big Thicket, it is one
of the easiest to visit and a good choice for families because of
the camping and tribal dances. Residents welcome visitors.

The reservation, straddling US 190 twenty miles west of
Woodville, has hiking trails and allows canoeing on the lake. A
small tourist complex is used for tribal dances, performed daily
in the summer for visitors.

The reservation lies in upland hardwood and pine forest and
is home to bobcats, coyotes, and armadillos. The southern edge
of the reservation forms a boundary with the northern edge of the
Big Sandy Creek Unit of the Big Thicket National Preserve.

History

The first European contact with the Alabama and Coushatta Indian tribes probably occurred in 1541, when Hernando de Soto's
men explored the rivers and creeks in what is now Mississippi.
Almost 300 years later, after Texas's War of Independence from
Mexico, Sam Houston rewarded the tribes for their participation
in the war by setting aside two tracts of land in East Texas as
reservations (by then the tribes had been forced westward out of
Alabama and Mississippi under pressure from settlers).

But political disputes with federal and local governments and lobbying by settlers prevented the Coushattas from moving onto their new promised land in Texas, and in 1858, they settled on the Alabamas' reservation. Later, in 1871, the two tribes joined forces and elected a single tribal chief to strengthen their political negotiations with government officials. By 1928, Sam Houston's original 1,110 acres had grown to 4,811 acres.

Recreation

The Alabama-Coushattas, unlike their greedier neighbors, have protected most of their land from development. As custodians of the ancient forest, the Alabama-Coushattas have resisted the temptation to reap quick profits from logging, and instead have chosen to balance economic necessity with preservation of the wilderness. The reservation is a small protected haven in the piney woods of East Texas. Visitors can take interpretive ecotours through the forest or hop into a boat and fish. If swimming and picnicking under the tall pines aren't enough, arrange at the visitors center to watch a traditional Indian dance or learn about tribal customs.

Where: Halfway between Livingston and Woodville on US 190.
Hours: Open daily year-round. Tours and tribal dances are suspended during December, January, and February.
Admission: No admission fee. Nominal fee for the nature tour and tribal dance. Separate nominal fee for campsites, to be paid at the general store near the entrance to the reservation.
Best time to visit: The weather is best in spring and late fall. Check the current weather forecast before heading out to the reservation.
Activities: Hiking, boating, fishing, swimming, nature bus tours, camping, and tribal dances. The Annual Pow-Wow, held in early June, is a treat for people of all ages.

Concessions: The reservation operates a small general store and tourist complex that is open to the public. A gift shop carries Indian handicrafts and exquisite hand-woven baskets sought by collectors. The restaurant caters to guests.

Pets: Permitted on a leash only.

Other: Bring your own wood for a campfire and generous amounts of mosquito repellent. If you're interested in the tribal dance, call ahead for a schedule.

For more information:

Alabama-Coushatta Indian Reservation, Route 3, Livingston, TX 77351; 800-444-3507.

MARTIN DIES JR. STATE PARK
and LAKE B. A. STEINHAGEN

Martin Dies Jr. State Park lies fourteen miles east of Woodville on US 190. This 705-acre park is made up of three independent tracts of land: the Cherokee Unit, Walnut Ridge, and Hen House Ridge. Walnut Ridge and Hen House Ridge lie on the eastern shore of the 15,000-acre Lake B. A. Steinhagen. The Cherokee Unit includes an island off the western shore of the lake and several narrow corridors of land across the lake.

Lake B. A. Steinhagen, created by impounding the confluence of the Neches and Angelina Rivers at Town Bluff Dam, is a center for water sports and naturalist activities. This park is popular with fishermen and boasts several fish-cleaning shelters. There are four boat ramps on the lake, and boat rentals are available on the western shore just south of US 190. Bird-watchers and campers enjoy the lakeside campsites and open forest.

On the north edge of Lake B. A. Steinhagen is the 4,042-acre Neches-Angelina State Wildlife Scientific Area, a swampland formed where the Neches and Angelina Rivers converge into the lake. It is accessible only by boat. Large numbers of alligators and wading birds can be seen year-round. Rookeries for anhingas, herons, and egrets provide scientists a chance to study the biology of these and 235 other bird species. This wetland on the northern edge of the lake is a maze of waterways through thick grasses, brush, willow trees, and water-tolerant hardwoods such as cypress.

Airboats are forbidden in the swamplands, and the rangers ask boaters to keep their distance from bird rookeries during nesting season so as not to upset reproduction patterns. One hundred of the bird species actually nest in the area, so bring binoculars.

A birding booklet for the park and surrounding areas is available at the entrance to Martin Dies Jr. State Park. Visitors may be lucky enough to see bald eagles, six kinds of woodpeckers, four types of owls, tundra swans, black-billed cuckoos, and vermilion flycatchers. The avian habitat of the state park includes lakeshore, slough, old-growth hardwood forest, and piney forest.

To the south of the park, south of Lake B. A. Steinhagen's Town Bluff Dam, is the Upper Neches Corridor Unit of the Big Thicket National Preserve.

Where: On US 190, halfway between Jasper and the intersection of US 190 and US 69.

Hours: Open daily year-round, except Walnut Ridge, which is closed in winter.

Admission: Nominal fee for entrance and camping.

Best time to visit: March to May and September to November. Winter freezes are not uncommon.

Activities: Bird-watching, boating, fishing, swimming, hiking, and camping.

Concessions: Ask at the park headquarters for directions to the nearest gas station and grocery store. Boat rentals are available, and there's one ramp in each unit of the park.

Pets: Dogs must be kept on a leash.

Other: At times it is very windy on and around Lake B. A. Steinhagen, a hazard for campers located near the water's edge. If you plan to camp, ask the rangers about the conditions on the lake. Boaters should be doubly careful not to exceed their skill limits. If you plan to visit the state scientific area, talk to the rangers at the state park first for hints on wildlife viewing and restrictions.

For more information:

Park Superintendent, Martin Dies Jr. State Park, Route 4, Box 274, Jasper, TX 75951; 409-384-5231.

BRAZOS BEND STATE PARK

High-pitched chirping sounds, a bit like a bird and a bit like a baby rabbit, carried on the breeze through the bulrush swamps at Brazos Bend State Park, where we were hiking. When we returned to the visitors center and reported the noise to the park ranger on duty, he sprang to action—with us and a half dozen other curious bystanders right behind.

Stepping warily into the swamp, he followed the sounds, and in a few moments emerged from the reeds with a basket of ready-to-hatch alligator eggs, which are slightly larger than chicken eggs.

Back at the interpretive center, one of the larger and better-staffed in the Texas State Park System, naturalists assisted the eager but impatient babies as they pecked away at the insides of their calcium homes. The eggs, said the ranger, had been laid and abandoned by a one-year-old female. Twenty-three minutes after they began to peep, three fat, yellow-green, striped alligators, each about nine inches long, were ready to take on the world. Just another day at Brazos Bend State Park.

The park, only fifty minutes southwest of Houston on the Brazos River, spans 4,900 acres of rolling, grassy savanna and

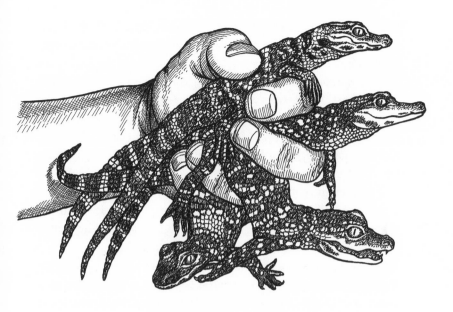

A handful of baby alligators greet the world

hardwood-palmetto forest, with seven big lakes linked by three winding bayous. In 1994, *National Geographic Traveler* magazine included Brazos Bend in its list of the nation's best state parks, and it is.

The Brazos River shifted course over thousands of years, leaving oxbow lakes that rise and fall with the rainfall and water level. Today these lakes and the mostly dry, occasionally flooded forest, reminiscent of East Africa's great national parks, make up Brazos Bend State Park.

Hiking and Bicycling

More than fifteen miles of hiking trails circle the lakes, and are easily accessible for hiking and mountain biking. Another big plus for fishing, bird-watching, and alligator spotting is the series of raised wooden platforms built on stilts on the shores of the lakes.

Ask about the following trails, which explore some of the park's most interesting areas: the 1.2-mile Forty-Acre Lake Loop, the 1.7-mile Elm Lake Trail, the 0.6-mile trail between Elm Lake and Forty-Acre Lake, the 1.6-mile Hale Lake Trail, and the one-mile Pliant Slough Trail. There are also four primitive trails totaling 8.5 miles.

Although mountain bikers are allowed on most trails, except during floods, hikers have the right of way. In addition, another twelve miles of park roads make for easy and enjoyable road biking and walking, except after it rains.

The best way to get to know the park is to start by walking around Elm Lake, the park's central lake. Large numbers of alligators live in this lake and spend most of their time lying up on the banks or floating motionlessly just below the water's surface, with only their eyes and snouts showing. In summer, giant water lilies blossom over the surface, turtles bask in the sun on dead logs, and jet-black anhingas perch on dead trees still standing in the middle of the lake.

For a longer hike, try the broad trail from Elm Lake northwest toward and around a set of small oxbow lakes. On the far side of the oxbow lakes, pick up a small path, partly overgrown with hip-high grasses, and continue north from the main loop back, which takes you out into the open savanna, dotted by live oaks draped in Spanish moss.

Three-foot-high fire-ant hills rising among the tall grass and rounded termite hills piled against fallen tree limbs are evidence of nature's constant efforts to recycle. The lacy webs of banana spiders stretch sixteen feet among low tree branches. Deer move quietly across the grassland and deep in the forest while coyotes and bobcats await the coming nightfall and the hunt for rabbits, squirrels, and field mice. Don't forget an insect repellent to fend off biting flies and mosquitoes, and sturdy shoes and heavy pants to protect against thick, thorny scrub and poisonous snakes. From here, the trail leads toward a small, narrow river valley.

The last time we hiked here, on the fifty-foot bluff above Big Creek, a half-dozen big alligators were sunning on the sandy banks. Then one by one they slithered into the river, snapping their tails as they hit the water. In a moment or two they surfaced, eyes and snouts just breaking the surface.

Another good hike is the loop trail around Forty-Acre Lake, starting from the parking area near the entrance. Halfway around the lake is a thirty-foot observation tower for wildlife spotting. Climb up and look for the roseate spoonbills, large wading birds that transform the surface of the lake from green to pink during peak nesting months in summer and fall. The pink tint, on the outspread wings of this large wading bird, dominates the scene. The spoonbill is often mistaken for the flamingo because of the vivid pink tint of its wing feathers and its unusually shaped beak.

The park's primitive trails, rarely used, go away from the lakes and creeks and down to the muddy Brazos River at the base of steep bluffs. Erosion from annual flooding has cut deep into these riverbanks.

Bird-watching

Bird-watchers can pick up a checklist at the park entrance. Compared with similar checklists from other Texas parks, we found it very complete, with information on which birds are seen during what seasons, their abundance, the best areas to expect sightings, and a notation on whether they nest at Brazos Bend. All this is preceded by a summary of the park's avian habitat. Up to 79 of the 274 different bird species sighted within the park are believed to nest here. There is also a large migratory population due to the park's location in a central flyway.

Astronomy

Brazos Bend State Park is the site of George Observatory, managed by the Houston Museum of Natural History. The observatory is usually closed during the day, but opens at night to the public, when the large white dome and its telescopes are popular for stargazing. Regular programs are hosted by the museum on the weekends, but if you're an astronomy buff, call ahead to arrange special viewing times. The observatory is located east of the interpretive center.

Where: Follow US 59 south for thirty minutes from Houston and across the Brazos River. Follow the signs south to the state park.
Hours: Open year-round; permits are required for overnight camping.
Admission: Nominal entrance and camping fee.
Best time to visit: Anytime, except winter.
Activities: Camping, hiking, fishing, bird-watching, astronomy, picnicking, backpacking, and mountain biking.
Concessions: None. The interpretive center has a small bookstore with limited titles.
Pets: Dogs must be kept on a leash.
Other: Follow the alligator etiquette rules noted in the handout you receive at the park entrance. Stay at least thirty feet away and do not annoy or throw things at them. Keep dogs on a short leash and do not allow them in the water, where hungry alligators have been known to attack them. Do not wade, swim, or play at the water's edge. Mosquitoes in Brazos Bend State Park seem

desperately underfed, so don't forget insect repellent. African bees, genetically pure killer bees, have been captured in bee traps near Houston. It might be wise to assume that the buzzing in the forest is not something you want to investigate personally.

For more information:

Park Superintendent, Brazos Bend State Park, 21901 FM 762, Needville, TX 77461; 409-553-3243.

THE NATIONAL FORESTS OF TEXAS

Only four national forests are located in Texas, all in the flat piney woods of East Texas. Totaling 634,849 acres, or almost 1,000 square miles, Sabine, Angelina, Sam Houston, and Davy Crockett National Forests encompass vast lakes, hundreds of miles of navigable rivers and streams, pine and hardwood forests, twenty-five established recreation areas, and over 200 miles of maintained hiking trails. The U.S. Forest Service, an agency of the U.S. Department of Agriculture, which has jurisdiction over the federal property, follows the government-mandated "balanced-use" approach to managing the forest resources. Logging, mining, oil production, and outdoor recreation are all sanctioned within the national-forest boundaries.

The logging and replanting of the forestland, which unfortunately favors the growth of single-species, commercially viable trees at the expense of native trees, which are not replanted, at least strikes a balance between complete protection on national park lands and no protection at all, the situation on most private land throughout the region. While any logging seems undesirable, without the management of the Forest Service, the local policy of clear-cutting would have meant the complete destruction of the forest.

A wide variety of commercial and recreational activities take place in Texas's four national forests, and the Forest

Service tries to cater to outdoor enthusiasts. Logging, oil exploration, and other kinds of natural-resource exploitation occur by permit only. Hunting season runs from October to January. Call the Forest Service to find out when the season opens and ends.

Over two dozen recreation areas have been established, ten in Angelina National Forest alone, creating opportunities to motorboat, canoe, fish, camp, hike, backpack, mountain-bike, study the wildlife, and picnic. You can hike and camp anywhere in the national forest, and since you are not restricted to staying on established trails or in primitive campsites or recreation areas, backcountry activities (cross-country hiking and backpacking) are popular (except during hunting season and the hot summer months).

Angelina National Forest

Spanning 154,244 acres, Angelina National Forest is the smallest of the four forests. Yet, because it surrounds the massive Sam Rayburn Reservoir, 114,500 acres with 560 miles of shoreline, along with the creeks and rivers that feed the reservoir, and the adjacent forests, Angelina has the largest number of developed recreation sites: ten within national forest boundaries, with an additional five on its perimeter.

After the Civil War, the lumber industry exploded in East Texas. The trees in this and the other national forests were heavily logged in the 1920s. In those days, logging companies were clear-cutting in such remote portions of the forest that they coined their own money and set up their own civil administration. Lumberjacks lived in the forest, cut off from family and friends for years on end. Since those days the pine woods in Angelina National Forest have made a surprisingly quick recovery, transformed into a wilderness area with a multitude of recreation possibilities.

The most-visited recreation areas are Townsend Camp-grounds, south of State 103, off FM 1277, and Caney Creek, east of Zavalla, off State 63 at the end of FM 2743. Both these recreation areas are located on the shores of Sam Rayburn Reservoir and offer boat ramps and large campgrounds. Caney Creek offers hiking trails and swimming. Both charge a nominal fee.

Where: Angelina National Forest lies east of the city of Lufkin and in portions of San Augustine, Nacogdoches, Jasper, and Angelina Counties. Contact the Forest Service Ranger District office for maps of roads and forest boundaries.

Best time to visit: September to June.

Activities: Camping, hiking, backpacking, fishing, swimming, boating, and wildlife observation.

Other: October through January is the hunting season, when off-trail hiking and backpacking are discouraged. In summer and fall, temperatures and mosquitoes are a problem, so most visitors prefer the recreation areas on the lake. Bring insect repellent. Contact the Forest Service for maps and directions to all recreation areas.

For more information:

Angelina Ranger District, 1907 Atkinson Drive, Lufkin, TX 75901; 409-639-8620.

Davy Crockett National Forest

At 161,500 acres, Davy Crockett National Forest is the largest and wildest of the four forests. Its northeastern boundary is the Neches River, which is fed by numerous tributaries. There are only five developed recreation sites, not so handy for car-campers, but great for backpackers and backcountry canoeists, who appreciate the forest's remote sloughs, bayous, and hiking areas.

Ratcliff Recreation Area, along Ratcliff Lake, is the busiest, for both day and overnight use in summer, although this is also the hottest time of the year. Located just west of Ratcliff on State 7, the recreation area offers both camping and hiking, including the trailhead for the twenty-mile Neches Overlook Trail, which winds eastward through the pine forest to the Neches River. Because of the distance, few backpackers, and even fewer casual hikers, are seen on this trail. Like all areas in the national forests, backpack camping is permitted anywhere.

To the north of Ratcliff is Big Slough, a winding waterway along the Neches. Here the Forest Service has established the Canoe Trail on Big Slough, the only canoe trail of its kind in southeastern Texas. Camping and fishing along the slough are popular, as are swimming, bird-watching, and picnicking.

Where: Davy Crockett National Forest is bounded by the cities of Crockett to the west, Lufkin to the east, Corrigan to the south, with the town of Alto to the north. Contact the Forest Service for maps.

Best time to visit: September to June.

Activities: Hiking, backpacking, camping, picnicking, canoeing, boating (no motors), fishing, swimming, and wildlife observation.

Other: October to January is the hunting season. Hiking and backpacking in the forest are discouraged during these months. In the summer, heat and mosquitoes can be a problem.

For more information:

Trinity Ranger District, State 94, Apple Springs, TX 75926; 409-831-2246.

Neches Ranger District, 1240 East Loop 304, Crockett, TX 75835; 409-544-2046.

Sabine National Forest

The 157,951-acre Sabine National Forest stretches along the western shore of Toledo Bend Reservoir, an impoundment of the Neches River that borders Louisiana. This national forest encompasses large tracts of woodland between the reservoir and San Augustine.

There are five established recreation areas in Sabine National Forest, the three most popular being Ragtown, Indian Mounds, and Red Hills Lake. Each has a boat ramp for fishing and wildlife observation. The campsites are somewhat limited, with both Ragtown and Red Hills Lake having only twenty-five sites each. Indian Mounds has over fifty sites. You'll find established hiking trails in Red Hills Lake Recreation Area, although hiking and camping are permitted anywhere on national-forest land.

Where: Sabine National Forest is east of San Augustine, north of the small town of Burkeville, south of the town of Joaquin, and bordered on the east by Toledo Bend Reservoir and Louisiana.

Best time to visit: September to June.

Activities: Boating, hiking, camping, swimming, fishing, backpacking, wildlife observation, and picnicking.

Other: Backcountry hiking and backpacking are discouraged during the hunting season, from October through January. Contact the Forest Service to find out when the season opens and closes. Mosquitoes can be a problem in summer and fall.

For more information:

Tenaha District, 101 South Bolivar, San Augustine, TX 75972; 409-275-2632.

Yellowpine District, 201 South Palm Street, Hemphill, TX 75948; 409-787-3870.

Sam Houston National Forest

The 161,154-acre Sam Houston National Forest lies between Lake Livingston and the city of Huntsville to the north, and is bordered by the city of Conroe to the south. The forest property includes vast, gently rolling pine woodlands, a portion of Lake Conroe, a state fish hatchery, a number of scenic areas, Huntsville State Park, and dozens of remote but navigable creeks and rivers.

The most popular destinations in this national forest include Huntsville State Park, Double Lake Recreation Area, Big Creek Scenic Area, and Stubblefield Lake Recreation Area. Hiking is very popular in the fall and winter on trails that cross each recreation area. Connecting these areas is the Lone Star Hiking Trail, a 140-mile trail that starts near FM 149, north of Montgomery, on the west side of the national forest, and runs eastward to Winter's Bayou Scenic Area. Individual hikers and backpackers travel portions of this heavily used trail throughout the year. Maps of the forest and the recreation areas are available from the Forest Service Ranger District offices.

Where: Sam Houston National Forest lies about an hour north of Houston and is bisected by I-45. It is bounded on the southeast by US 59 and is south of the city of Huntsville.

Best time to visit: September through May, although it is best to avoid venturing out into the backcountry during hunting season, from October to January.

Activities: Camping, fishing, hiking, boating, swimming, backpacking, picnicking, wildlife observation, and mountain biking.

Other: Since the national forests are multiuse areas and hunting is permitted from October through January, hikers and backpackers are discouraged from entering the backcountry.

For more information:

San Jacinto Ranger District, 308 North Belcher Street, Cleveland, TX 77327; 713-592-6461.

Raven Ranger District, FM 1375, New Waverly, TX 77358; 409-344-6205.

4

The Upper
Texas Coast

INTRODUCTION

More than thirteen parks and wildlife refuges stretch along
Texas's Upper Gulf Coast, 200 miles of sandy shoreline that runs
from the mouth of the Sabine River on the Louisiana border to
the bay at Corpus Christi. It was here, in 1900, on these shores
and coastal prairies, that the most deadly hurricane in North
American history swept ashore, claiming more than 6,000 lives.

If you believe in legends, pirate Jean Lafitte's fabled treasure lies buried somewhere along the coast. But digging for
the gold is not allowed, since the parks and refuges, managed
jointly by the Texas Parks and Wildlife Department and the U.S.
Fish and Wildlife Service (U.S. Department of the Interior), are
protected under the Coastal Barrier Resources System Act of
1982.

The National Wildlife Refuge System was created almost a
century ago, in 1903, by President Teddy Roosevelt, himself a

hunter, who realized that the breeding grounds of native North American birds, whose numbers were dwindling even then, needed to be protected.

By protecting the habitat, Roosevelt's action helped save many mammals and reptiles as well. Today, in the Texas parklands, the population of the previously endangered American alligator has rebounded from an all-time low in the 1960s to a present count of over 150,000 in the Lone Star State alone.

Along the upper Texas coastline, wildlife viewing and birding are probably the most popular outdoor pastimes in the refuges. The marshlands are home to javelina (whose closest relative is the South African peccary), mink, river otter, bobcat, the hybrid red wolf-coyote, the endangered whooping crane, and one of the most diverse avian populations in the United States. More than 300 resident and migratory bird species have been identified.

Largely due to Roosevelt's intervention, the upper Texas coast often leads the National Audubon Society's annual winter bird census count, a measure of the number of species sighted in twenty-four hours in a given 7.5-mile radius. The city of Freeport, in fact, holds the national record at 226 species. Serious birders can expect to see more than 100 species on an average day during the winter migrations, and in spring, large flocks of birds, weary from their flight across the Gulf from Central and South America, blanket the coastal marshlands to rest and feed.

While wildlife observation is the main attraction, many visitors escape for weekends to the coast for fishing, sunbathing and swimming, shell collecting, boating, and camping. Almost everyone who comes to the coast ends up planning a return visit to these white-sand beaches. With water temperatures between 70° and 80°F, the Gulf waters offer a welcome respite from the 100° heat and high humidity typical of Southeast Texas in summer.

Anhingas swim with only their heads above water, dive to catch a fish, and then toss it up in the air to swallow it

Occasional hurricanes and tropical storms lash the shore-line, bringing both destruction and rebirth of the coastal ecology. Beach sand and lagoon silt are redistributed, sandbars destroyed and reformed, dunes reshaped, and new lakes and channels formed. In the aftermath of these destructive storms, new com-munities of vegetation sprout from the sand in the tidal zones, and mammals, birds, and amphibians again take up their places in the cycle of life.

Miles of uninhabited coastal flatlands stretch from the shoreline inland through forests and pasturelands. Bayous and rivers, winding like ribbons toward the Gulf, inch lazily over the landscape. The silt washing downstream from the Sabine, San Bernard, and Brazos Rivers builds and restores the barrier islands, turning bayous into lakes and fringing them with bul-rush, cordgrass, and saltgrass.

Whether you're skimming across tidal marshes on an "everglade" airboat, paddling a canoe through brackish back-waters, or driving along embankments in these wild parklands, the wild and very accessible Texas coastline offers endless out-door opportunities.

SEA RIM STATE PARK

Sea Rim State Park, with 15,109 acres and more than five miles of coastline, protects the state's finest example of native sea rim marshes and the barrier islands that they eventually become.

The park, nine miles west of Sabine Pass and the Louisiana border, and between the Intracoastal Waterway and the Gulf of Mexico, is divided into two units on either side of State 87: the Beach Unit along the Gulf shore and the Marshlands Unit along the Intracoastal Waterway.

As the Sabine River flows into the Gulf, moving at the rate of 510 cubic meters per second, its silt-laden water is carried westward by strong currents, eventually forming dunes along the Gulf-side shoreline and brackish marshes on the inland side of the barrier island. As silt accumulates, the marshes gradually stabilize and evolve into coastal prairie, and the barrier island grows larger.

Raised wooden walkways built over the marshes give visitors a chance to examine at close range the specialized cordgrass and saltgrass habitat that has adapted to daily fluctuations in the salinity of the water.

Beach Unit

The park headquarters, located at the entrance to the Beach Unit, provides a trail guide to the Gambusia Trail, a wheelchair-accessible interpretive nature walk. This trail, a 3,640-foot-long raised boardwalk, begins at the end of the parking lot and juts out into the marshland, winding its way through the cordgrass. If you look down into the marsh water, you can see the gambusia, for which the trail is named, one- to two-inch-long fish that feed on mosquito larvae. Nutria and muskrat, the marshland's two largest mammals, build dens similar to beaver lodges, only smaller and made of grass. Their homes rise several feet above the surface of the water in the middle of the marshes. Nutria and muskrat are rarely seen during the day but occasionally appear at dusk to feed. After sunset, venture quietly out on the boardwalk with a flashlight and inspect the dens. You may also find raccoons, which climb up on the boardwalk to shell and eat crayfish.

Miles of shorefront sand dunes in the Beach Unit offer swimming, sunbathing, and windsurfing. Campgrounds, located behind the dunes and protected from the water, are adjacent to the interpretive center and park headquarters in the Beach Unit.

Start your visit at the interpretive center, where exhibits and photographs describe the sea rim marsh habitat.

Marshlands Unit

The best camping and wildlife observation in the park are in the Marshlands Unit, north of State 87. Serious wildlife watchers and those in search of solitude wind up in this little-visited part of the park. Accessible only by boat, the unit has four observation platforms, five geographically separated camping platforms, and numerous fishing and crabbing locations. Before heading out into the Marshlands Unit, you need to file a float plan with park headquarters in the Beach Unit.

Few experiences parallel a night or two camping on a platform deep in the marsh. From late afternoon through dusk, mink, river otter, raccoon, and nutria come out to feed. As the sun sets, birds chirp noisily in the thick grass. The moon rises to the trills and croaking of insects and frogs, and stars twinkle overhead as the ocean breeze carries away the heat of the day.

Alligators are common in the park and eat just about everything, from frogs, fish, and snakes to raccoons. Keep an eye out for them, especially if you're in a boat that tips—a canoe or pirogue. The cottonmouth water moccasin is another unwelcome inhabitant.

If you don't camp on a platform, the next best thing is an airboat ride through the marsh, one of the finest ways to see the relatively inaccessible backwater areas. The airboat, typically a flat-bottom raft with an airplane propeller attached to an automobile engine, glides effortlessly across the top of shallow water and marsh grasses. The ride takes you through a series of open lakes and predefined airboat paths (to minimize environmental impact).

Bird-watching

Migratory and nesting waterfowl are best viewed in the fall and winter, although certain park areas are closed during nesting season. Nearly 290 bird species have been spotted in the park, and 28 species nest here, including the uncommon yellow-billed cuckoo. Routine sightings of bald eagles, ospreys, caracaras, peregrine falcons, hawks, and kites in the park are a thrill even for experienced birders.

Where: Located west of Sabine Pass on State 87. Follow the signs to park headquarters and the entrance to the Beach Unit and the Marshlands Unit.

Hours: Daily year-round. During the annual migrations in winter the Marshlands Unit closes to visitors.

Admission: Nominal entrance and camping fees.

Best time to visit: March to June and September to November. November is the wettest month. July is the hottest, with average high temperatures above 90°F.

Activities: Hiking, boating, wildlife observation, bird-watching, swimming (not in the Marshlands Unit), camping, and fishing.

Concessions: A concessionaire provides airboat rides into the Marshlands Unit from March until October. Check with park headquarters for the latest fees. Canoe rentals are available near the entrance to the Marshlands Unit.

Pets: Allowed only on a leash in the Beach Unit. Not permitted in the Marshlands Unit.

Other: Due to extremely hot, humid weather and the slow-moving marsh water, be prepared for mosquitoes. If you plan on camping in the Marshlands Unit, take with you the water you'll need.

For more information:

Superintendent, Sea Rim State Park, P.O. Box 1066, Sabine Pass, TX 77655; 409-971-2559.

McFADDIN NATIONAL WILDLIFE REFUGE

McFaddin National Wildlife Refuge, west of Sea Rim State Park along State 87, surrounds 41,682 acres of intertidal marshland with wildlife viewing opportunities that rival those at Sea Rim.

Unlike the latter, however, McFaddin has a number of trails and roads that cross deep into the refuge, making it easy to explore on your own. According to the U.S. Fish and Wildlife Service, one of the state's largest alligator populations lives here, as do various small mammals, including fox, bobcat, and mink.

Use the eight miles of roadways along the embankments beside the marshes to get from the highway into the refuge. Developed campgrounds, picnic areas, and swimming beaches are located along the Gulf shore, where the water temperature in summer hovers around 80°F. Three boat ramps have been installed for fishermen trailing dinghies and motorboats.

Multipurpose trails on raised land above the marshes make it possible to walk almost everywhere in the refuge, which is probably the best way to see animals and birds. Wear heavy hiking boots for muddy trails, and take insect repellent to ward off mosquitoes. Since the refuge is open only during the week, it is one of Texas's least crowded.

Where: Follow State 87 west from Sabine Pass. Look for signs to McFaddin once you've passed Sea Rim State Park. Or follow State 87 east from the Galveston–Port Bolivar Ferry to the refuge entrance.
Hours: Open weekdays from dawn to dusk. Overnight camping is permitted in the Gulf shore campgrounds.
Best time to visit: March to June and September to November.
Activities: Boating, fishing, wildlife observation, bird-watching, and camping.
For more information:
    Refuge Manager, McFaddin National Wildlife Refuge, P.O. Box 609, Sabine Pass, TX 77655; 409-971-2909.

ANAHUAC NATIONAL WILDLIFE REFUGE

Established in 1963, Anahuac National Wildlife Refuge protects a varied community of wildlife that inhabits mixed brackish marsh and wetland prairies east of Galveston, on the east side of East Bay.

Because the 28,506-acre refuge is only an hour's drive from Houston, it is one of the most visited on the upper Texas coastline. Twelve miles of gravel and hard-packed oyster-shell roads allow driving or walking through the wetlands, for close-up viewing and photographing of animals and birds. Mountain bikers, always looking for off-road trails, have discovered the refuge, although the ride is sometimes pretty rough. Boaters and fishermen can put into the bay at ramps near the park entrance and along the shore of East Bay. To limit impact on the wildlife, boating on inland waterways is not allowed, except on the boat canal near the entrance and along Oyster Bayou, a channel that enters the bay.

Bird-watching

Of the 268 bird species identified at Anahuac, about 255 are permanent residents, including the large-beaked belted kingfisher, roseate spoonbill, iridescent blue gallinule, and masked duck. To date, forty-one species have been counted nesting within the refuge.

During the annual winter migrations, from November through March, flocks with up to 50,000 snow geese descend on the fields and ponds at Anahuac. From March onward through spring, the salt-cedar trees lining the east edge of Salt Cedar Road are alive with the chirping of songbirds.

Farther south toward East Bay, the marsh itself is usually dotted with wading spoonbills, storks, ibis, and egrets, while pelicans, cormorants, and other diving birds fish along the bay shore. Hawks and kestrels circle and soar overhead, and in late summer, when the refuge waters reach their lowest levels, vultures appear on exposed sandbars to scavenge for dead and/or stranded fish. Bald and golden eagles, caracaras, and ospreys arrive through fall and winter.

Mammals and Alligators

While mammals are common throughout the preserve, you aren't likely to spot them until after dusk. Then, a drive through the refuge may yield glimpses of muskrat, mink, river otter, and nutria. Bobcat sightings are rare, although their spoor is an indication of a healthy population.

The best time to see alligators is on the first warm days of spring, when dozens of these cold-blooded amphibious reptiles climb up on the dry banks of cordgrass to soak up the sun. You're almost guaranteed to see some on the shores of Shoveler Pond, in the waterways along Teal Slough Road, and along Salt Cedar Road.

Later, during the hot summer months, when the water levels in the marsh drop, the alligators dig deep sinkholes, where they wait for the rainy days of fall. When the rains finally arrive, the sinkholes become small ponds for fish and waterways for otter and mink.

Wildlife Conservation

Striking a balance in the refuges among farming, grazing, hunting, and protecting native habitats hasn't been easy. Alhough most of the original coastal prairie land in Texas is now gone, the ideas on how private and public land should be used are so strong that the U.S. Fish and Wildlife Service has had to accommodate all points of view.

Limited hunting and fishing are permitted, but the revenue from the sale of hunting tags and licenses pays for conservation programs. More than half of Anahuac Refuge was acquired with fees from the sale of federal duck-hunting stamps. Moreover, most hunters now realize that for their sport to continue, protecting healthy bird populations and their habitats is vital. Some 12,000 acres within the refuge are completely closed to the public year-round, except during waterfowl hunting season.

Action by conservation organizations came too late for some animals native to the Gulf. The endangered red wolf is now extinct in the wild because of hunting, loss of habitat, and hybridization with coyotes. Red wolves trapped in the 1970s at this wildlife refuge have undergone successful breeding programs and are being reintroduced in the Carolinas, and biologists hope they can be reintroduced here as well.

Where: Take I-10 east from Houston to FM 562 south. The refuge is eighteen miles south of I-10. Take FM 562 to FM 1985, and follow the signs to the gravel road entrance.

Hours: Open year-round, dawn to dusk, except for overnight campers.

Admission: No fees, but you are asked to log in your visit at the kiosk near the entrance.

Best time to visit: Spring and fall. The best bird and wildlife viewing is in early morning and evening.

Activities: Hiking, camping, wildlife observation, bird-watching, fishing, and boating.

Concessions: None. The closest gas stations and food stores are in Anahuac and Stowell, over thirty minutes from the refuge.

Other: Camping is permitted on the shore of East Galveston Bay, but is not encouraged by the refuge management and is limited to three nights. There are no developed facilities or fresh water.

For more information:

Refuge Manager, Anahuac National Wildlife Refuge, P.O. Box 278, Anahuac, TX 77514; 409-267-2337.

GALVESTON ISLAND

Galveston Island is the most developed of all Texas's barrier islands, with towns, beaches, resorts, water sports, shopping, and parks. Starting in the spring and continuing through the fall, the island, located forty-five minutes south of Houston at the end of I-45, is packed with weekenders and vacationers from all over Texas.

Galveston Island, originally inhabited by Indians (who were thought to be cannibals) and later by the Spanish and French, has now grown from a hideaway for Jean Lafitte and his pirate band to a crowded and bustling resort and recreation area. Expensive restaurants cater to well-heeled visitors, and a spate of Victorian homes have been given a face-lift.

After the 1900 hurricane, when a twenty-foot tidal surge and 100-mile-per-hour winds destroyed most of the buildings, people thought Galveston was finished. But a protective seawall was erected, and the town was rebuilt.

Moody Gardens

Located at the northern edge of Galveston Island, Moody Gardens is an entertaining weekend destination for families with children. Self-guided walks tour the distinctive ten-story glass Rainforest Pyramid, a greenhouse for more than 1,000 unusual and rare plants, insects, birds, and fish from tropical rainforests around the world. You'll also find an IMAX theater, freshwater swimming lagoons, convention center, Japanese gardens, Hope Rose Garden, and walking paths.

The exotic vegetation isn't arranged according to region, but mixes species from South America, Central America, Central Africa, Southeast Asia, and the Indian Ocean region in imaginative ways.

Deep purple orchids dangle from tree limbs, bamboo stalks rise skyward, and over 100 different palm species transport you from Galveston to the heart of the jungle. Bromeliads bloom year-round in the humid environment, and tropical butterflies flit from blossom to blossom.

Five different ponds inside the pyramid are home to over ten different species of rare tropical fish, including mudskippers, Mexican blind cave fish, and various cichlids. End your visit in the movie theater, which shows 3-D IMAX movies on a giant screen.

Where: Moody Gardens is near the north shore of the island. Take I-45 south and exit on 61st Street, after crossing the Intracoastal Waterway. Turn right on Seawall Boulevard and right again on 81st Street. Turn left on Hope Road to the entrance.
Hours: Open daily from 10:00 A.M. to 10:00 P.M.
Admission: There is an entrance fee to the Rainforest Pyramid and the 3-D IMAX theater.
For more information:
Moody Gardens, 800-582-4673.

Underwater Adventure

Local dive shops in Houston and Galveston swear that the best scuba diving in the Gulf of Mexico is found right here in Texas at the Flower Gardens, about 100 miles southeast of Galveston Island. This reef system of tropical corals and fish rises to within sixty feet of the ocean's surface and covers nearly 500 acres comprising two distinct and different sections of seafloor (one 400 acres in breadth and the other 100 acres).

Although the Flower Gardens are actually more than 300 miles north of the tropics, at least 18 kinds of tropical corals and 175 fish species thrive in the Gulf. Commercial oil exploration has been prohibited in the immediate area (although, sadly, oil is being pumped not too far away), and the Flower Gardens are being considered for status as a national marine sanctuary.

The Flower Gardens are a remote destination best suited for advanced divers able to cope with the long ride to the site, occasional rough seas, and strong currents. Once in the water, however, divers will find the gardens are a fantasy of colors and shapes, with living coral, brightly colored fish, and schools of manta rays.

Multiday diving trips can be arranged though dive shops in Freeport and Galveston. Shorter day trips can be arranged to offshore oil derricks and sunken boats. Be aware that all dive trips in the Gulf require a long boat ride, usually through rough seas kicked up by strong winds. Most divers use scopolamine patches to prevent motion sickness. For a list of charter companies with live-aboard boats and certified dive outfitters, call the Galveston Convention and Visitors Bureau.

For more information:

Galveston Convention and Visitors Bureau, Moody Civic Center, 2106 Seawall Road, Galveston, TX; 409-763-4311.

Galveston Island State Park

This 1,950-acre park, six miles from Galveston, north of FM 3005, stretches over 1.5 miles of sandy beach, sea rim marsh, and dunes. During the summer, the picnicking facilities and outdoor amphitheater attract large crowds of parents and children, while the beach is crowded with swimmers, sunbathers, and beachcombers.

Though campers quickly fill the campsites on the weekends, most visitors are here on day outings, from the Hill Country, Dallas, Fort Worth, and Houston. The park, consequently, is one of the state system's busiest.

Four miles of nature trails explore the dunes and marshes, where tens of thousands of migratory birds settle on parkland after their flight across the Gulf. Winter and spring mornings are the best times for bird-watchers, especially after a cold front has passed through and birds driven south fill the marshes.

Two observation platforms and five bird blinds have been erected for wildlife viewing. Ask at the information station for a bird checklist and about recent sightings.

Where: Follow FM 3005, from Seawall Boulevard in Galveston, southwest six miles to Park Road 66, which leads to the entrance.

Hours: Open daily.

Admission: Nominal entrance and camping fee.

Best time to visit: Spring and fall. Good weather is also possible in winter, but so are cold fronts and rain. Summer is generally hot and humid, but with a constant onshore breeze.

Activities: Hiking, camping, swimming, picnicking, and bird-watching.

For more information:

Park Superintendent, Galveston Island State Park, Route 1, Box 156A, Galveston, TX 77554; 409-737-1222.

BRAZOSPORT AREA NATIONAL WILDLIFE REFUGES

If the heat and humidity on the Gulf Coast really get to you, consider including the Brazoria National Wildlife Refuge and San Bernard National Wildlife Refuge, along the marshy coast of Brazoria and Matagorda Counties, in your plans.

Along this section of coastline, watered by the Brazos, San Bernard, and Colorado Rivers, unusual weather patterns off the Gulf of Mexico interact with mainland weather to produce delayed seasonal effects. When summer has arrived elsewhere, it is still spring in both refuges and cool enough for comfortable fishing and birding.

Later in summer, biting insects at both refuges are an irritant and a blessing. By August, they can make a visit almost unbearable. But it is the insects, at the bottom of the food chain, that make these refuges so ideal for the complex ecosystems they nourish.

Fish, birds, and small marsh animals dine on insects, while wading birds prey on small fish. Larger raptors eat not only the fish but smaller birds and reptiles, which also serve as dinner for small mammals, snakes, alligators, and turtles. Both refuges have a diverse animal population, including many (rarely seen) bobcats and river otters. Coyotes and raccoons, usually nocturnal, often emerge in early evening. Alligators are common, and the rangers say that a large population of cottonmouth water moccasins and pit vipers live in the marshes, although visitors rarely see them. If you hike off the trails, to be on the safe side, watch where you step and wear sturdy boots.

Don't be surprised to see cattle, which are currently being allowed to graze here in the refuges on select tracts to remove thick underbrush, as part of the long-term management goals to encourage the return of migratory birds. The hybrid Indian Brahman/Angus (Brangus), which thrives well in the intense heat and humidity, does a good job of clearing non-native underbrush and improving the prairie habitat for birds and small mammals. In addition, controlled burns are scheduled periodically to remove dry underbrush.

Water levels in the ponds and swamps are maintained through a series of dikes, in an effort to re-create the environment here before settlers began cultivating and ranching the area. The new, balanced marshland habitat supports 273 bird species, many reptiles, and large mammals.

To explore the lakes and bayous at Brazoria and San Bernard, you can put in a boat at ramps installed in both refuges; or you can reach both refuges from the Intracoastal Waterway. Fishermen have illegally erected one-room shacks on stilts in the marshy swamps near the refuge borders. While they are still sometimes used, the U.S. Fish and Wildlife Service plans to tear them down.

Brazoria National Wildlife Refuge

On a typical early winter morning, a group of birders makes the ten-mile trek east out of Freeport to the 40,854-acre Brazoria National Wildlife Refuge to catch one of the most unusual sights in North America: a gaggle of 100,000 migrating geese, ducks, and other waterfowl at their ancestral winter home, a land of meandering bayous, oak woodlands, sea rim marshes, coastal prairie, and mudflats.

Six miles of gravel road provide excellent access to this marvelous refuge, where prairie lands are vast rookeries and alligators lie up on the cordgrass banks, close to the water. From all sides comes a constant chorus of chirping, peeping, whistling, and chattering, the accumulated music of seventy-one bird species nesting in the refuge.

While you'll see birds and wildlife at any time of year, late winter and spring are when the migratory species are in residence, resting, feeding, and nesting. And four endangered birds are regular year-round visitors: brown pelicans, peregrine falcons, whooping cranes, and bald eagles. Binoculars are a must.

Where: Ten miles east of Freeport, south of FM 2004. Take FM 2004 to County Road 227 and the entrance.
Hours: Open only the first full weekend of every month, dawn to dusk. Tours and access can be arranged for any time of the month by contacting the refuge manager.
Admission: No fee.
Best time to visit: November through April. Be prepared for unpredictable weather.

Brown pelicans are making a comeback in the Gulf states

Activities: Bird-watching, wildlife observation, hiking, fishing, and nature tours.

Concessions: None.

Other: During the spring and summer mosquitoes and biting flies make visiting the refuge uncomfortable. Remember to take a DEET-based insect repellent. On especially bad days when you need extra protection, spray permethrin on your clothing.

For more information:

Refuge Manager, Brazoria National Wildlife Refuge Complex, P.O. Drawer 1088, 1212 North Velasco, Angleton, TX 77516; 409-849-6062.

San Bernard National Wildlife Refuge

The 24,455-acre San Bernard National Wildlife Refuge, twenty minutes west of Freeport, is another excellent bird-watching site. A small, one-room visitors center at the refuge entrance supplies maps and information about this wilderness area along with general information on the National Wildlife Refuge System, the marshland habitats that support the bird populations, and fishing and hunting regulations.

The refuge lies in an intertidal zone, from roughly three feet below sea level to about nine feet above sea level. In Cow Trap Lake, which is usually a swampy marsh just below sea level, cordgrass and mud marshes predominate, while live oaks and willows grow on the higher ground near the refuge entrance.

You can pick up a bird checklist for both the Brazoria and San Bernard Refuges at the headquarters. At least fifteen raptor species have been identified here. Near the entrance of the refuge, live oaks and willows support a large passerine (perching bird) population.

Although the refuge has quite a large mammal population, these animals are not normally out and about during the day.

If you know what to look for, however, you'll see bobcat and coyote tracks and droppings throughout the refuge. River otters are also common in the waterways but seen even more rarely.

Live oyster beds in the Intracoastal Waterway have created shallow reefs that support redfish, black drum, speckled trout, and flounder. Anglers fish from the shoreline with long poles, their lines stretching far out into the water. Fishing, crabbing, and shrimping are popular pastimes.

Where: The refuge is ten miles west of Freeport off County Road 306. With a good map and a boat, visitors can also make their way into the refuge by water.

Hours: Open daily, dawn to dusk.

Admission: No fee.

Best time to visit: October to March, though winter weather can be unpredictable.

Activities: Hiking, mountain biking, bird-watching, wildlife observation, fishing, and boating.

Concessions: None.

Other: Bird-watchers can arrange for special tours given by the refuge staff.

For more information:

Refuge Manager, Brazoria National Wildlife Refuge Complex, P.O. Drawer 1088, 1216 North Velasco, Angleton, TX 77515; 409-849-6062.

ARANSAS NATIONAL WILDLIFE REFUGE

Bring a camera and tripod to the Aransas National Wildlife Refuge, the cornerstone of the National Wildlife Refuge System, which protects the sandy shores, sea rim marshes, coastal prairies, and oak woodlands of Blackjack Peninsula and Matagorda Island.

Aransas, just forty-five minutes east of Corpus Christi, is known across America as the last home of the endangered whooping crane, a situation the refuge officials are doing their best to change. The calls of the whooping crane and other birds can be heard in the marshland. On Matagorda Island, endangered sea turtles lay their eggs along the shoreline. White clouds and blue skies provide a backdrop for circling bald eagles.

Interpretive Center

On your way into this coastal wilderness stop at the Wildlife interpretive center, which we think is the largest and best-staffed refuge center in Texas. The park staff asks you to register upon arrival and offers printed information on local birds, reptiles, and mammals. In addition to wildlife viewing at the refuge, you can hike, fish, picnic, or attend nature programs. There is more here, actually, than you can see or do in a single day.

A small but well-stocked book section sells titles on the ecology, flora, and fauna of Aransas, and outstanding exhibits offer a key to identifying javelinas, wildcats, snakes, and other park species. For bird-watchers, a checklist of 389 identified species is available.

Scenic Drive and Wildlife Observation

A paved road, starting near the Wildlife interpretive center, circles through the refuge for sixteen miles. Stop at the promontory overlooking San Antonio Bay and Mustang Lake, where a tall concrete observation platform has been erected. Climb to the top and look through the pedestal-mounted telescope to see thousands of roseate spoonbills, whooping cranes, and other waterfowl wading in the marsh at the lake's edge. The telescope also

**Peccaries or javelinas prefer cactus, especially prickly pear,
which provides water as well as food—they even eat the spines**

picks up other distant wildlife: a raccoon at the water's edge and
sometimes dolphins in the bay.

From Mustang Lake the road curves inland through a
thicket of live oaks, then out across open prairie, where shallow
gullies, dry grass, and thickets of brush and trees provide homes
for many of the refuge's mammals. Deer, mountain lions, bobcats, rabbits, and rodents have all been identified in the refuge.

Turning north, the road leads through semitimbered grasslands: keep an eye peeled for groups of javelinas moving through
the underbrush. In spring you'll often see the newborns hovering
under the legs of their parents. Wild boar and feral hogs, both introduced species, have resisted all efforts to remove them and
are, at least for now, a permanent part of the Aransas menagerie.

During the spring and fall, look for the large Mexican free-
tailed bats, which migrate through the refuge and can be seen at

dusk hunting for insects. You can recognize them by their over-sized wingspread and the rapid, erratic movement of their wings. Three other bat species are also common in the refuge — the Georgia, red, and silver-haired bats.

Sometimes mistaken for bats are common nighthawks, which swerve, climb, and turn, also hunting insects at dusk. These birds, once mistakenly thought to feed on the blood of animals, earned the colloquial name *goatsuckers*. Whippoorwills and pauraques, also goatsuckers, are common in Aransas.

Hiking

Driving through the refuge is the most convenient way to see the park, but hiking gets you up close and personal. Six separate walking trails combine for a level 4.3-mile route. The Rail Trail and the Heron Flats Trail, which start and end near the Wildlife interpretive center, take you through the refuge's swampy lowlands, where alligators bask in the sun and a constant onshore breeze provides relief.

The Big Tree Trail, Boardwalk, and Hog Lake Trail all begin and end near the base of the observation platform, crossing through an ancient live-oak forest, across marshlands, and around the lake.

Where: The refuge is just forty-five minutes east of Corpus Christi, off State 35. Follow the signs to the refuge entrance.
Hours: Open daily, dawn to dusk. The Wildlife interpretive center is open from 8:30 A.M. to 4:30 P.M.
Admission: No fee.
Best time to visit: October to April, since this is the winter home of the whooping crane. Spring and summer are also good, since the coastal climate moderates the otherwise hot temperatures.

**Rare whooping cranes winter among sandhill cranes
along the Texas Gulf Coast**

Activities: Bird-watching, hiking, picnicking, fishing, and wild-life observation.

Concessions: None. The Wildlife interpretive center has a small selection of books.

Pets: Must be kept on a short leash.

Other: Poisonous snakes and alligators live in the refuge. Swimming is not permitted. Insect repellent is a good idea. Deer and javelinas regularly wander the roadways, so avoid speeding.

For more information:

Refuge Manager, Aransas National Wildlife Refuge, P.O. Box 100, Austwell, TX 77950; 512-286-3559.

5

Tropical Texas

INTRODUCTION

Tropical Texas? Well, not exactly, but almost. The southernmost point along the Rio Grande dips to within 2.5 degrees of the Tropic of Cancer, the boundary of the tropics. Easterly winds blowing over the Gulf of Mexico and heavy moisture-laden air from Bahia de Campeche mix with a turbulent intertropical convergence zone to create hot, sultry conditions ripe for summer thunderstorms and hurricanes.

The Rio Grande Valley, where a mix of vegetation zones along the riverbanks between Falcon Reservoir and the coast ncludes thorn-tree savanna, lush riparian forests, and irrigated farm fields, is a habitat for animal species normally found in the tropical forests of Central America. The parks and refuges here were created to protect the unique ecology of the river valley and its animal and plant life, and to provide recreational opportunities to hike, camp, boat, and, most of all, observe the diverse wildlife.

The lower Rio Grande and Texas shoreline are for those

looking for a true wilderness experience. People of any age or physical ability can stalk the elusive jaguarundi or ocelot with a camera, fish in the intertidal zone, canoe on the Rio Grande, bird-watch at national wildlife refuges, or hike in the half-dozen parks.

On Padre Island, a barrier island stretching 113 miles along the length of the South Texas shoreline, hot winds blowing off the Gulf shape and reshape the sand dunes. Black mangrove thickets, rarely found outside the tropics, flourish in the intertidal zones of lagoons and bays along the Intracoastal Waterway. These were the waters once sailed by ships of the Spanish Main.

Inland, away from the Gulf and north of the Rio Grande, thorny forests and acacia trees dot dry lowlands. If you've seen the grassy savannas of East Africa, this area of South Texas will bring back memories. Remember that backcountry forests and preserves pose hazards. Visitors wandering off trails are likely to encounter poisonous toads, African bee colonies, poisonous plants, and the standard fare of snakes and insects.

Geologic forces during the Cretaceous period began the chain of events that created this blend of tropical vegetation, barrier islands, and savanna. Once submerged under shallow seas, the plains and rolling lowlands of Texas's deep south were formed as the result of successive sedimentation, tectonic movements, and receding oceans. This is the only area in Texas where rocks and formations from the seven most recent geologic eras emerge at the surface. Other than volcanic eruptions, this represents the most recent geological formation in the United States.

MUSTANG ISLAND STATE PARK

The slightly salty, onshore ocean breeze cools the hot, humid summer days on Mustang Island. Often described as one of the nation's best beaches, this 3,703-acre state park sports 7,000 feet of shoreline for camping and another 14,000 feet of open dunes and shell-speckled white sands.

Visitors, lured by swimming, sunbathing, camping, and fishing, find the windy shores of this barrier island near Aransas and Corpus Christi, and only four hours from Houston, a welcome weekend retreat. Steady winds and waves create challenging conditions for windsurfers and good sailboating weather. Boaters and fishermen should follow the access road to the bay side of the island, where there are launch ramps for motorboats and sailboats. Tankers on the distant horizon, flickering in the heat waves, are a reminder that this is also a commercial body of water.

Sand-Dune Ecology

The fragile, constantly shifting sand dunes on the island form the basis of a unique biotic zone. Rising thirty-five feet from sea level on the Gulf side of the island, these dunes support animal and plant life adapted to survival in the windy, salty environment. On the bay side of the island, the tall dunes fade away into flat salt marshes characterized by salt-tolerant grasses and plants. Dense bulrush (a cousin of the Egyptian papyrus) and cattail stands grow in depressions fed by rainwater.

The Texas Parks and Wildlife Department has declared the dunes off-limits for hiking, since footprints can upset the natural balance of wind, salt, and rainwater. Any changes in freshwater supplies causes increased salinity, which kills off the plant life and drives away animals and birds. It can take months to reestablish the ecological balance in the damaged dunes before they can again support plant and animal life.

Thriving vines and plants bring the hot, sandy desolation to life. Stroll along the base of the dunes and look for bird, reptile, and mammal tracks. It soon becomes apparent that the plant life offers not only a source of food and water, but also shade, to lizards and other reptiles under the hot sun. The plant life anchors the dunes, allowing them to grow with the shifting and blowing sand.

Bird-watching

Mustang Island, like most of the barrier islands and estuaries between Corpus Christi and the Louisiana border, is alive with the flapping and squawking of both winter and spring waterfowl and passerines. Unseasonable spring cold fronts dip south, driving birds hundreds of miles outside their normal ranges to parks along the coast, like Mustang Island. In the fall these cold fronts signal the onset of winter and the annual migrations. Out of the 164 species listed on the bird checklist (available from the park rangers), 117 are migratory.

Mustang Island, unlike the rest of Texas's southeast coast, is cooled by a steady onshore breeze in summer and reaches into the sixties and seventies in winter, and is consequently a favorite destination for wildlife viewing.

Where: The park is south of Port Aransas and across the bay from Corpus Christi. The park can be reached by taking the toll-free ferry from Aransas Pass to Port Aransas and following the signs south on Park Road 53. If coming from Corpus Christi, take the bridge to Padre Island and follow the park road north to Mustang Island.

Hours: The park and campsites are open daily. RV sites with hookups are available. Primitive camping is permitted along beaches where there are no established sites; just pitch your tent at the base of the dunes. Campers will find the entrance gates locked late at night, so if your plans call for a late arrival, call ahead for the gate combination.

Admission: Nominal fee.

Best time to visit: March through October. Winters can be blustery and the weather unpredictable.

Activities: Camping, boating, beachcombing, swimming, fishing, and bird-watching.

For more information:

Superintendent, Mustang Island State Park, P.O. Box 326, Port Aransas, TX 78373; 512-749-5246.

PADRE ISLAND NATIONAL SEASHORE

The sun never really rose on August 10, 1980, over 113-mile-long Padre Island off the Texas coast. On that historic day, Hurricane Allen swept over the world's longest barrier island, bringing 115-mile-per-hour winds and a 12-foot tidal storm surge, while cyclonic storm clouds overhead stretched from Missouri and Oklahoma deep into Mexico and as far west as the Big Bend on the Rio Grande.

By the time the eye of the storm had passed and the torrential rains and floods subsided, the state's most expensive natural disaster had done an estimated $600 million in damage and written itself into the history books.

On Padre Island, of which eighty coastal miles are designated as national seashore, the hurricane was just one of many environmental events that have shaped the evolution of this national treasure. Long-shore currents, the deposition of silt from the rivers that empty into the Intracoastal Waterway, and strong onshore winds throughout the year continually shape and reshape the island.

Recreation

Warm Gulf waters, bright sunny days, and isolation have made this island a haven for outdoor recreation. Boats ply the waters in Laguna Madre, a lagoon between the barrier island and the mainland. The park offers surfing in the Gulf, beachcombing, fishing, hiking, and picnicking. Four-wheel-drive vehicles are permitted to drive south across the sandy beaches, but not in the dunes, where tire tracks destroy the fragile dune ecology.

To camp in the wild "down-island" end of Padre Island, ask the rangers for advice. Their suggestions will help you find the fastest way to put distance between you and the crowded and commercial north end of the island. At the south end, fifty-five miles of isolated beach are available for beachcombing, fishing, swimming, or napping beneath an umbrella.

Camping is allowed anywhere along the edge of the dunes. From June through August, you may see the endangered Kemp's ridley sea turtles, Atlantic green sea turtles, and loggerhead turtles emerging from the surf to dig their nests, lay their eggs, and return to the ocean. At night, between the occasional yip-yip of a coyote and the incessant crash of the waves, this is a very nice place to be lulled to sleep.

Sport fishermen come from all over the country to cast from the surf for redfish, speckled sea trout, and occasionally a hammerhead shark or black-tipped shark. In Laguna Madre, use a boat to catch flounder, red drum, and sheepshead.

History

Padre Island has a long and colorful pirate history embroidered with the legends and stories of rogue ships and shipwrecked Spanish galleons stranded on hidden sandbars. Pirate Jean Lafitte's fabled treasure is rumored to be here, somewhere, along with millions in gold and silver coins from long-lost galleons. Metal detectors are illegal on the island, but visitors still hope that the wind may shift the sand just enough to unearth buried treasure.

Wildlife Observation

The real treasure of Padre Island is equally compelling: the riches of a protected natural wildlife community far from civilization, where you can camp in the wilds and observe wildlife in their native habitat. Keep in mind that there are no gas stations or restaurants within the national seashore and freshwater is not available south of the park's established campsites. You must bring your own.

Wildlife observation opportunities throughout the island include five different types of rare sea turtles (Kemp's ridley, leatherback, hawksbill, Atlantic green, and loggerhead). During the summer, beginning in May, volunteer turtle patrols roam the beaches tagging and counting the turtles. For the last decade, conservation efforts jointly sponsored by the National Park Service and private conservation groups have been trying to increase the number of sea turtles that nest on the island. Most efforts are being focused on the Kemp's ridley sea turtle, which is being reintroduced to the island.

Even though over thirty snake species live in the marshlands and dunes, poisonous snakes, including rattlesnakes, are uncommon. From the shore you may also see the dorsal fins of Atlantic bottle-nosed and spotted dolphins — not sharks — cutting through the water. Threatened peregrine falcons migrate through the area in September.

In early summer, Portuguese men-of-war, blue jellyfish between six and twelve inches long, wash up on the beaches. This jellyfish, with a distinctive wavy "sail" that makes it easy to recognize, is very poisonous. Measured gram for gram, the jellyfish poison is as dangerous as a cobra's venom, and on rare occasions has killed small mammals. Residents along Texas's coastline usually carry meat tenderizer to put on a sting for relief — the enzymes digest the proteins in the poison.

A special program to save Kemp's ridley turtle is based in Galveston

Seashell Collecting

If you've seen the largest seashell collection in Texas at the Houston Museum of Natural Science, you'll be interested in shell collecting on the beaches of Padre Island, where shells ranging from a few millimeters to a foot or more in length come in all shapes, sizes, and colors. The National Park Service allows beachcombers to take what they find as long as it is not alive or of historical interest, a departure from almost every other national park. The best time for shell collecting is in the aftermath of strong storms, when rigorous wave action washes them up on the beach.

Children are thrilled to discover a whole auger shell, lined tulip shell, or giant Atlantic cockle shell. Bring a trophy bag to put them in, but check to make sure the shells are uninhabited. Collecting live shells is illegal.

Education Programs

The park rangers offer a number of programs for people of all ages, from the junior seashore ranger program (for children ages five to thirteen) to the nightly education programs for all ages at Malaquite Beach. The evening slide shows at the amphitheater help orient visitors to the seashore's surroundings. A schedule of events is available from the visitors center.

   While at the beach watch out for too much sun. The rangers advise you to wear a hat and sunscreen, not only to protect you from a sunburn, but more important, from heat exhaustion. Pamphlets at the entrance station remind visitors that rattle-snakes, though rare, do live on the island.

Where: From Corpus Christi, cross the bridge to Padre Island, turn south on Park Road 22, and go to the north beach entrance. From the Aransas National Wildlife Refuge, take State 35 south to Aransas Pass, cross the Intracoastal Waterway by ferry to Port Aransas, and follow Park Road 53 south along Mustang Island to Park Road 22 south to the national seashore.
Hours: Open year-round. The visitors center is open daily, closing early at 4:00 P.M. in winter.
Admission: Nominal fee for entrance, additional fee for camping.
Best time to visit: April through October. The hurricane season starts in June and runs until November. Summer temperatures are hot, but rarely climb over 90°F in the day and 80°F at night.
Activities: Camping, hiking, beachcombing, fishing, swimming, and wildlife observation. Backcountry camping is allowed by permit only. Permits are issued at the ranger station.

Concessions: Near the visitors center you'll find a snack bar and gift shop.

Other: Campgrounds are open daily and are available on a first-come, first-served basis. Boat launching is permitted year-round from the Bird Island Basin ramp.

For more information:

Padre Island National Seashore, 9405 South Padre Island Drive, Corpus Christi, TX 78418; 512-937-2621.

LAGUNA ATASCOSA NATIONAL WILDLIFE REFUGE

Laguna Atascosa National Wildlife Refuge, established in 1946, is the largest protected parcel in the lower Rio Grande Valley, encompassing 45,000 acres of virgin shoreline habitat. Less than five percent of the original habitat in the Rio Grande Valley remains today; the rest has been cleared, irrigated, and plowed into fields.

The refuge, within what biologists call the "Tamaulipan biotic region," which stretches as far north as Mustang Island, is on the mainland side of the Intracoastal Waterway, west of South Padre Island and east of Harlingen off FM 106.

Because Laguna Atascosa, or "muddy lagoon," receives only twenty-six inches of rain annually, it harbors both subtropical and semiarid vegetation zones. Portions are heavily wooded while other areas are grassy coastal prairie.

The intertidal vegetation zones have their own unique ecology. Stop by the interpretive center to learn more about Laguna Atascosa's biodiversity before setting out on the refuge's fifteen-mile self-guided driving tour, which follows a well-graded dirt road through coastal prairie to the edge of Laguna Madre.

Visitors to the refuge can hike, picnic, fish out of the ship channel, and, as in all other national wildlife refuges, come for the bird-watching.

Bird-watching and Wildlife Observation

With 394 species, Laguna Atascosa is one of the most popular birding destinations in Texas. As you enter the refuge, stop to pick up a checklist from the interpretive center. Even those with little interest in bird-watching are struck by the refuge's sheer number and variety of avian species.

You can see the refuge on a driving tour, starting at the visitors center, stopping at the Redhead Overlook viewing platform, and moving from one habitat to another. During annual migrations, thousands of sandhill cranes blanket the refuge flatlands.

The best time of the year for wildlife viewing is winter through midsummer, when cranes, ducks, and other migrating waterfowl winter in and near the refuge from November to February. Songbirds migrate through the refuge in April through June, and species from Mexico—green jays, white-tipped doves, and chachalacas—frequent the refuge from May to August.

Though birds are the main interest in Laguna Atascosa, a sizable population of mammals also resides in the park, about thirty species. The heavily wooded portions of the refuge provide a home for several wild cats—ocelot, bobcat, and jaguarundi. Occasionally mountain lions are seen in the park. Deer and javelinas are commonly seen on the driving tour, especially at dusk along the roads.

Plant Life

The shoreline here supports well in excess of 600 plant species, some extremely rare and found only in restricted areas, a number of them being tropical intertidal plant species found nowhere else in Texas. Mangroves, far north of their normal range, cling to life along the lagoons and inlets. On the fringes of the lagoon itself, look for the six- to nine-foot black mangrove trees and their distinctive roots that rise up out of the soil to about six inches. If there hasn't been a freeze in several years, look for the small red mangroves that support themselves on a tangle of above-ground roots. Unfortunately the red mangrove does not generally do well in Texas due to the cold winters.

Where: From Brownsville, follow FM 1847 north through Los Fresnos and on to the north entrance to the refuge. To get to the south entrance and the interpretive center, follow FM 106 east of Rio Hondo and look for the signs to the entrance.

Hours: Refuge tour roads open daily, dawn to dusk. The interpretive center closes for the summer, from June through August, is open only on weekends in September and May, and is open daily from October to April.

Admission: No fee.

Best time to visit: October through April. Many prefer the off-season months of September and May.

Activities: Wildlife observation, picnicking, and fishing out of the ship channel.

Pets: Permitted only on a leash, but be courteous to bird-watchers and keep dogs at a distance.

Other: This refuge is intended for wildlife observation. All other recreational activities are prohibited. Closest accommodations are on South Padre Island, in Rio Hondo, or in Harlingen. Camping is available in Adolph Thomas Jr. County Park.

For more information:

Refuge Manager, Laguna Atascosa National Wildlife Refuge, Box 450, Rio Hondo, TX 78583; 210-748-3607.

SANTA ANA NATIONAL WILDLIFE REFUGE

The boisterous call of a chachalaca isn't something you'd expect to hear in Texas. Nor is the cooing of the Inca dove or the cheeping of the green parakeet. But in the 2,080-acre Santa Ana

National Wildlife Refuge, established in 1943, these birds and others, including three species of native parrots and the exotic military macaw, treat visitors to a chorus of screeching and squawking.

Santa Ana's main attraction is wildlife observation, especially birding, by tram, by car, or on foot. There isn't much else to do, but most visitors don't find this a problem because of the refuge's biodiversity. What there is here in this small refuge on the banks of the Rio Grande keeps people coming back.

Why are there so many birds at Santa Ana? Because two major North American bird migration flyways, the Central and the Mississippi, converge along the lower Rio Grande, and the refuge lies in the path of both, between the banks of the Rio Grande and near US 281, between Harlingen and McAllen. At least 377 species regularly visit the refuge and have been identified.

Visitors Center

The visitors center is the jumping-off point into the refuge, for both families and bird-watchers, with cameras and binoculars in hand. Visitors hope to learn about the rare ocelot and the refuge's unusual plant life. Guided tours in the facility-operated tramcars leave the headquarters at regular intervals.

On display inside the visitors center are samples of the silky pelts of the wild cats of Santa Ana: ocelot, jaguarundi, bobcat, and mountain lion. The spotted ocelot fur coat resembles that of a small cheetah, and the unusual reddish-brown coat of the jaguarundi is colored for camouflage.

A large, well-documented display on African bees describes their habits, origin, and how to avoid becoming their victim. By early 1994, these aggressive bees made up over 30 percent of the bee population in the river valley (something to think about when you hear buzzing in the forest). By 1995, up to

80 percent of the bee population in the river valley is expected to be Africanized.

Information pamphlets from the visitors center also describe how to recognize the presence of the area's three ants: large, red, stinging harvester ants; fire ants; and leaf-cutter ants. In the auditorium you can view an audiovisual show on the unique river biota, and satellite photographs on the walls highlight the vegetative zones in the valley in shades of green and brown, showing a slowly degrading and disappearing ecology. There is virtually no preservation of habitat on the Mexican side of the river.

Refuge Drive and Hiking Trails

After you've seen the displays and exhibits in the visitors center, head out into the refuge itself, where you can hike, drive your car, or take a guided tour on the refuge trams, a seven-mile route deep into the forest. When the trams are running during peak visiting months, the road is closed to private cars.

If you have the stamina, stick with the hiking trails, a better way to see things close up. The park's eleven hiking trails, totaling twelve miles, are open from sunrise to sunset. The main trailhead is past the giant palmetto tree outside the visitors center.

Before setting out, check with the rangers about taking safety precautions. While the river valley area is the only place in Texas without rattlesnakes, there are other hazards: mosquitoes, biting ants, scorpions, poisonous giant toads, poisonous coral snakes, and thorny plants.

For the best backcountry experience, fill your water bottle, lather up with mosquito repellent, and venture out into the heavily canopied forest on the two-mile Wildlife Management Trail. Listen for the screeches of the chachalaca and see (and hear) bees building nests in the upper branches of the trees.

From the dimly lit forest floor below, you can hear birds fluttering up in the tree canopy. Through the foliage comes the hornlike call of the giant toad, and Mediterranean geckos and the threatened Texas indigo snakes line the vines and trees. Follow the trail through the tall grasses, circling Pintail Lake until you meet a bend in the Rio Grande. The cliffs overlooking the river are unstable, and every year a few people end up on the riverbanks after the sandy bluffs collapse.

To get away from people, try hiking on the Jaguarundi Trail, a round-trip hike of over five miles that starts at a cutoff from Trail B. Walk along Trail B until it crosses over a small creek, then look for the cutoff where the Jaguarundi Trail splits off to the south. The path is infrequently used and usually overgrown, so you may have to spend a moment searching for the trailhead. Follow it for two miles, crossing several other trails heading down to the river, in one of the most remote areas of the refuge. The park staff strongly recommends not leaving the trails or trying to walk cross-country since it is easy to lose your way in the dim forest. To get back to the visitors center, retrace your steps, or follow the trail back from the river to the refuge road and then follow the road back to the trailhead.

Bird-watching and Wildlife Observation

Whether you see the park by car, trail, or interpretive tram, any visit will be rewarded with the sights and sounds of the tropical forest habitat. Dozens of types of birds can frequently be seen, especially from photography blinds and the network of trails winding into the interior. Of the nearly 400 species of birds seen in the river valley region, at least fifty are of special interest to birders, including the Aztec thrush, the green jay, and the gray-crowned yellowthroat.

The plant, mammal, and reptile populations are almost as

diverse as that of the birds, and perhaps even more appealing (though don't suggest this to a serious birder). The checklist at the visitors center lists forty-two mammals, twelve amphibians, and thirty-four reptiles. Five species are on the endangered list, and six more are considered threatened.

Where: Drive east on US 83 from McAllen. Six miles out of town, pick up FM 907 south to US 281. Drive east and follow the signs to the entrance.

Hours: Open year-round from sunrise to sunset except Thanksgiving, Christmas, and New Year's Day. Refuge Drive is closed from June through August, when the refuge tramcars operate tours. (Private cars are allowed on Refuge Drive except when the birds are breeding and nesting or when the tram is in operation. Call the refuge for details before setting out.) The parking lot of the refuge is open from sunrise to sunset.

Admission: No entrance fee, nominal fee for refuge tram tour.

Best time to visit: Any time of the year. In summer, be prepared for wet weather and hot, sultry conditions. In winter, the temperatures vary widely. Wildlife observation, photography, and identification are good year-round.

Activities: Wildlife observation. Biking is permitted on Refuge Drive but not on the trails.

Pets: Must be on a leash at all times.

Other: Picnicking and feeding the wildlife are prohibited. Camping is not allowed in the refuge. The nearest campsites are in Bentsen–Rio Grande Valley State Park.

For more information:

Refuge Manager, Santa Ana National Wildlife Refuge, Route 2, Box 202A, Alamo, TX 78516; 210-787-3079.

BENTSEN–RIO GRANDE VALLEY STATE PARK

This is not a big park by any stretch of the imagination, but what the Bentsen–Rio Grande Valley State Park lacks in space (it is only 588 acres) it makes up for in subtropical vegetation, wild-life, and birds. To get there, follow the signs west out of McAllen on US 83 and south toward the Rio Grande. This jungle-like forest provides opportunities to camp, canoe, bird-watch, and track wildlife.

Animals

In the early mornings, look for cat tracks along the paths, the prints of ocelots, bobcats, and jaguarundis, animals rarely seen during the day. Their tracks and spoor are the only evidence most people will see of these cats. If you hike on the trails at dusk, with a flashlight, and remain quiet, you may catch a glimpse of these animals.

There is relatively little danger from snakes, despite their presence. The only poisonous snake, the coral snake, is rarely seen. Other snakes include the indigo snake (usually found far-ther south in Mexico) and the bull snake. Rattlesnakes are almost nonexistent, kept in check by the indigo and bull snakes, which compete for the food supply.

When hiking you may see giant toads, up to seven inches long. Don't pick them up, because they have specialized parotid glands, which squirt poisonous secretions harmful to other animals. The giant toad is related to the cane toad in Australia, with poison glands strong enough to kill a dog. Also common in the park are javelinas, seven species of bats, and countless cotton and rice rats (an important food source for the cats and snakes).

If you see a trail of green leaves walking upright across the forest floor, you have spotted a colony of harmless leaf-cutter ants at work. Leaf-cutter ant hills are most often found in well-drained, moist soils, in contrast to the large, red, biting harvester ants, which prefer arid soils. Both are common in the park; all ants should be left alone.

Bird-watching

Like Santa Ana National Wildlife Refuge, this is also an internationally known birding destination. Also, like Santa Ana and Laguna Atascosa, it is one of the few protected natural areas in the Tamaulipan biotic region, with 296 species listed in the bird checklist. Birds unique to the biota of the Rio Grande include the pauraque, green jay, groove-billed ani (a member of the cuckoo family), tropical parula, chachalaca, and ferruginous pygmy owl.

Plants

Unusual plants include the coyotillo, a tropical shrub common to Central America, whose berries, when eaten, cause paralysis of the arms and legs; the sweet acacia with its yellow-orange flowers; the white-flowered catclaw acacia; and the Texas ebony tree, with its white flowers contrasting against its deep green foliage.

The park spans two different vegetation zones. Near the river, the lush riparian forest, almost jungle-like, is marked by rare tropical plants and vines. Away from the river, the South Texas subtropical thorn scrub and mesquite chaparral can at times be impenetrable.

Hiking

Two hiking nature trails wind through the forest, allowing visitors to see the park up close. The vegetation is so aggressive that without constant maintenance the forest would quickly reclaim these trails. Pamphlets describing the trails and the park's two major habitats, riparian woodlands and subtropical thorn woodlands, are available at the entrance station.

The first trail is the Singing Chaparral Trail, a one-mile loop that winds through thorny vegetation typical of South Texas's chaparral. The second trail, the Rio Grande Hiking Trail, a 1.8-mile loop, swings down to an overlook bluff on the river where you can see the subtropical riparian vegetation on the banks of the muddy Rio Grande.

Be careful when following the trails to stay on the path. In places the forest canopy blocks the sun so completely that it is possible to get lost in the tangle of trees, vines, and shrubs. Thorn-plant thickets can quickly become a painful irritant.

Recreation

To enjoy the park from the water, launch a canoe in the park's oxbow lake, adjacent to the camping sites. This lake, a meander of the Rio Grande that was cut off and isolated, is filled with bass and catfish suitable for a fish-fry on the park's grills.

Bentsen–Rio Grande Valley State Park, six hours from San Antonio and eight hours from Houston, is a good place for campouts for scout troops, families, and individuals interested in experiencing the out-of-doors in an unusual subtropical setting. The park's relative isolation and uncrowded campgrounds make it an enjoyable overnight weekend spot.

Where: Follow US 83 west from Harlingen and Brownsville toward Mission. Exit south on Loop 374 and follow FM 2062 south to the park entrance.
Hours: Open daily year-round.
Admission: Nominal entrance and camping fee.
Best time to visit: Spring and fall. The warm climate makes visiting in winter also enjoyable. Avoid July and August, when the temperatures average between 90° and 100°F. The wettest time of the year is September and October. Heavy rains can flood the campsites.

Activities: Wildlife observation and photography, fishing, boating, camping, and hiking.

Pets: Permitted only on a leash.

Other: The hot, humid climate in the river valley is perfect for mosquitoes. Remember to bring plenty of insect repellent. Locals use the park and its sixty-acre oxbow lake, on the border of the park, for fishing and boating.

For more information:

Park Superintendent, Bentsen–Rio Grande State Park, P.O. Box 988, Mission, TX 78572; 210-585-1107.

SABAL PALM GROVE SANCTUARY

The 172-acre Sabal Palm Grove Sanctuary is six miles south of Brownsville where Texas dips to its farthest point south. Nestled into a meander of the Rio Grande, the park is on lush, forested flatlands bordering the muddy river. The Sabal palm, an endangered species for which the sanctuary is named, used to cover vast areas in the lower Rio Grande Valley, but today, the palm groves are almost gone. With the palms covering about thirty acres, the rest of the sanctuary is ex-farmland that is gradually reverting to natural woodlands and wetlands. Other vegetation of interest besides the palm groves includes the Texas ebony tree and thorn scrub brush.

The sanctuary, managed by the National Audubon Society, is also a protected habitat for nearly 400 tropical and subtropical bird species. A bird checklist and other information pamphlets on the sanctuary are available from the visitors center near the entrance.

Through efforts to protect the palm grove, other endangered animal and plant species have also benefited. Ocelots and jaguarundis are regularly spotted here, although other wild cats, such as the margay and the jaguar, which used to prowl this area, were eliminated long before the sanctuary was established.

The rings, stripes, and spots on the ocelot vary from cat to cat

A one-half-mile self-guided nature trail winds through the palm grove, starting near the sanctuary entrance. An interpretive booklet, available from the visitors center, describes the plant and animal life around you at each of the trail markers. After seeing the palm grove, explore other areas in the sanctuary. Once you've seen the farmlands that are being allowed to revert to their natural state, you'll have a better idea of the damage done when natural plants are cleared, plowed under, irrigated, sprayed with insecticide, and fertilized.

Although this is the smallest of all the natural areas in this book, any visit to the Deep South would be incomplete without stopping at the Sabal Palm Grove Sanctuary.

Where: From Brownsville, follow State 4 east to FM 3068. Turn south and then west on FM 1419 to the entrance.
Hours: In winter, November through April, the sanctuary is open from Thursday through Monday. From May through October, the sanctuary is open only on weekends.
Admission: Nominal fee.
Best time to visit: November through April, before the summer heat sets in and the bird population is at its maximum. The heat and humidity of summer, though, are offset by the change in the number and types of birds.
Activities: Bird-watching, botany, and interpretive trails.
Other: Bring insect repellent to ward off mosquitoes and biting flies.
For more information:
Refuge Manager, Sabal Palm Grove Sanctuary, P.O. Box 5052, Brownsville, TX 78523; 210-541-8034.

6

The Panhandle
and North Texas

INTRODUCTION

While the parks and wildlife preserves in East and South Texas
seem to steal most of the thunder, northern Texas, the most
densely populated area in the state, also has a number of smaller,
though less well known, wilderness areas. Most are popular as
weekend destinations.

North Texas, stretching from the Louisiana border to New
Mexico, is a varied collage of wildlife habitats, vegetation zones,
and geologic formations, with an equally diverse group of animal
and plant species. Recreation includes camping, hiking, birding,
and horseback riding.

In the northwest, the Panhandle's Caprock Escarpment, a
high ridge that runs north to south, divides the Panhandle in two.
(The escarpment is also referred to as the Llano Estacado, or
Staked Plain.) To the west of the Caprock ridge are the dusty, flat
High Plains, at an elevation of about 3,100 feet.

Eastward are rolling grassland prairies, about 1,200 feet lower in elevation. Where the High Plains meet the prairies, a series of wild and sculpted canyonlands are dotted with parks, wildlife refuges, and hilly grasslands, all rugged and remote.

In the 10,000 years since the Pleistocene era, when the Panhandle was much wetter and giant bison and mastodon roamed the area, both wind and rain have eroded the uplifted plains, carving hills and canyons.

Tributaries of the Red, Brazos, and Colorado Rivers continued the erosion, cutting the 1,000-foot-deep canyons of today's Palo Duro and Caprock Canyons State Parks.

In north central and northeastern Texas, around Dallas and Abilene, parks and wildlife sanctuaries occupy the prairies and forests where the once-vital cattle industry followed the Chisolm, Western, and Shawnee Trails to market.

In prehistoric times, the land now within Dinosaur Valley State Park was once ocean bottom and swamps, where dinosaurs lived in the marshes and mudflats bordering what is now the Gulf of Mexico. In 1993, the park's collection of preserved dinosaur tracks and fossil bones attracted 312,000 visitors.

The northeastern area is characterized by lakes and rivers suitable for boating, fishing, and canoeing. Caddo Lake State Park, on the Texas-Louisiana border, has the state's finest tupelo and cypress swamplands, a premier place to canoe. A large bird population also attracts bird-watchers and campers.

Four little-known national grasslands totaling over 100,000 acres are scattered across northern Texas, divided into dozens of separate administrative sectors. By 1895, cattle grazing and farming on the native grasslands had exhausted the thin topsoils, which dried, cracked, and blew away in annual dust storms. Today, one hundred years later, under federal management, the national grasslands are being restored for both wildlife protection and recreation.

Buffalo herds still graze the Texas prairie

PALO DURO CANYON STATE PARK

Palo Duro Canyon State Park, 16,000 acres enclosing a 120-mile-long canyon with 1,200-foot-high walls, was carved by a powerful river, the Prairie Dog Town Fork of the Red River. Along the canyon walls dinosaur fossils have been exposed over time, showing that the plateau was once a swampland. The area was inhabited as long as 12,000 years ago, as tools and weapons for hunting giant bison and mastodon indicate.

In the last century, in 1874, the U.S. Army rode into Palo Duro Canyon, where the Comanches had holed up, and, in the last great Indian battle fought in Texas, defeated them and drove them out of the canyon.

The park entrance and visitors center, twenty-two miles southeast of Amarillo, sit high on the crest of the Caprock. The center houses exhibits on the geology and history of the region, and sells books and maps. From the entrance, the park road passes a canyon overlook—stop for the views—and then descends to the valley floor, to hiking trails, stables, and campgrounds.

The river and abundant wildlife in the canyon bottom made this area a favorite hunting ground not only for the Cheyenne tribe, but also for Kiowa, Apache, and other Indian tribes, and it is still a wonderful place to hike, camp, explore, and look for wildlife.

There are both primitive campsites for tent campers and sites that include electrical and water hookups. In summer, the park's 1,742-seat amphitheater is busy on weekend evenings with musicals and theater productions.

Wildlife Observation

Deer and bobcats are common in the canyon, and mountain lions frequent the most isolated and rugged corners of the canyon. Occasionally the roar of the large cats echoes down and around the canyon's cliffs, a thrilling noise. Coyotes, ringtails, raccoons, porcupines, and foxes also live in the park, and there is a large population of African aoudad sheep, imported into Texas but released into the wild.

Occasionally pronghorn antelope are seen wandering through the canyon. At dusk beaver now frequent the riverbanks. More than 200 bird species live within the protection of the canyon walls, where food and water supplies are plentiful. A list of identified birds includes various hawks, golden eagles, crows, blackbirds, vultures, and wild turkeys.

**Pronghorn antelope, the Western Hemisphere's fastest animal,
can achieve speeds of up to seventy miles an hour**

Hiking and Horseback Riding

Hikers can try the Lighthouse Trail, the park's one maintained
trail, or can venture off cross-country. The Lighthouse Trail, an
easy walk that leads to a scenic view of a water- and wind-eroded
geologic formation that resembles a lighthouse, is 4.6 miles

round-trip. To head out cross-country, pick up a map at the visitors center, and plan your hike. There are nearly fifty miles of unimproved trails, and you are allowed to hike anywhere. The map is sufficient to navigate you through the park's wilderness without getting lost. Horseback riding, also permitted in the park, can be a great way to cover large distances under the hot summer sun.

Our two favorite walks are down the river at sunset (you'll be surprised at the amount of wildlife you'll see along the water's edge) and a rock scramble in any one of the smaller canyons. If you can climb to the top of Mesquite Mesa, in the center of the park, there's a wonderful view of the canyon up and down river.

The footing in the long, jagged canyons on the mesa's south side is tricky, but hiking in the most remote part of the park is rewarding, especially in spring, when wildflowers blanket the mesa. The mesa's soft limestone cliffs crumble easily, so watch your step. If you choose a long hike into the southern part of the park, check in with the rangers, tell them your plan before you go, and report back afterward (otherwise they may send out a search party).

Guided Tours

An easier way to sightsee is a ride on the Sad Monkey Railroad's miniature train along a two-mile route on the canyon floor. From the train you'll get spectacular views of rock formations and an Indian pictograph site. The tour guide and train conductor points out some of the curved, windblown rock formations that have been named after things they resemble, like the Lighthouse, Sad Monkeys, and Santana's Face.

Where: Located south of Amarillo. Follow I-27 south from the Amarillo city limits to State 217. Take State 217 east to the park entrance.

Hours: Open daily year-round.

Admission: Nominal entrance fee, additional fee for campsites.

Best time to visit: April through October. The summer months are the most popular. Between late October and mid-April the temperatures regularly dip below freezing, and winter weather can be harsh.

Activities: Camping, hiking, horseback riding, wildlife observation, and bird-watching.

Concessions: The Goodnight Trading Post, a general store, sells food and necessities.

Pets: Horses are permitted on equestrian trails. Call park headquarters for information on local horse rental companies. Horses are not permitted in the park overnight.

For more information:

Park Superintendent, Palo Duro Canyon State Park, Route 2, Box 285, Canyon, TX 79015; 806-488-2227.

CAPROCK CANYONS STATE PARK

Caprock Canyons State Park, established in 1975, is about one and a half hours south and east of Palo Duro on I-27 and State 86. This park, at 13,906 acres, is not quite as large as Palo Duro but is the result of the same geologic forces. Its steep, craggy canyons and rugged cliffs are etched in the plateau of the High Plains. Rows of convoluted arroyos are carved by four tributaries of the Little Red River: the North Prong, the South Prong, Holmes Creek, and Mule Creek.

The canyons, plunging 1,000 feet from the rim of the High Plains, form a natural wildlife viewing area. Equidistant from Lubbock and Amarillo, this park is one of the wildest and least visited in the Panhandle.

In one corner of the park is 120-acre Lake Theo, for boating, fishing, and swimming. Other recreation includes horseback riding, mountain biking, hiking, and bird-watching. On summer evenings, nature and history programs are given at the park's modest amphitheater.

History

Caprock Canyons has a rich history of human habitation. Folsom points, dating 10,000 years ago and fashioned from Alibates flint (the quarry is located 130 miles north, near the Canadian River), have been recovered from a suspected Folsom culture camp on the south shore of Lake Theo. Stone scrapers and bones indicate that people of this age hunted and tanned bison hides and were seminomadic. Piles of ancient animal bones have also been found elsewhere in the canyons, suggesting the area was well populated.

When the first Europeans crossed this region in the 1540s, the area was populated by Kiowas and Plains Apaches. Trade with the Spanish introduced horses to the Apaches, who quickly became efficient buffalo hunters and followed the annual buffalo migrations.

Several hundred years later, in the 1700s, the aggressive Comanches drove out the Plains Apaches, and in the late 1800s the U.S. Army Cavalry and settlers defeated the Comanches. By then, though, the buffalo were gone, the countryside fenced, and cattle ranching was decimating the native grasslands.

Wildlife

Most visitors to the park make a point of trying to see the park's herd of wild pronghorn antelope and a buffalo herd, the largest in the Texas state park system. Beaver have made a tremendous comeback and are thick in the streams and rivers. African aoudad sheep flourish as well, and golden eagles spiral on thermal currents high overhead.

The birding list, available on entering the park, lists over 175 species living in a variety of habitats. According to the rangers, a number of different vegetation zones can be identified in the park, from the High Plains prairie, where moderate rainfall supports short grasses and shrubs, to semiarid badlands with cacti and thorny mesquite.

Woodlands occupy the drier hillsides, forested in oaks and cottonwoods, and in bottomland valleys long-stem grasses and a variety of trees grow along creeks and rivers, the best habitats for birds.

Hiking and Horseback Riding

Over 5,000 acres in the park are dedicated to trail riding and saddlepack camping, with corrals, hitching posts, and a developed equestrian campground. A backcountry campsite, the Equestrian Primitive Area, is available for those who like to trail-ride and camp out under the stars in the backcountry.

Sixteen miles of challenging hiking trails climb through the canyons formed by the North Prong and South Prong Rivers, short trails with sometimes steep elevation gains and sun exposure. The longest trail in the park, the ten-mile loop trail, starts at the Little Red Camping Area and makes its way in a broad circle through the arid chaparral. Several other shorter trails cross through the same area, better suited for half-day hikes. Cross-country bushwhacking is allowed, and a map is available on entering the park.

Biking

County Road 1065, which runs north-south through the eastern third of the park, is the only access to the eight-mile-long Mountain Bike Trail that weaves its way along Mule Creek and then crosses over to the Little Red River. Biking is permitted on all trails, at your own risk, but check at park headquarters for trail conditions, weather, and restrictions.

Where: The park is located equidistant from Amarillo and Lubbock on I-27. Follow State 86 east from I-27, past Silverton, to the park entrance.

Hours: Open daily year-round.

Admission: Nominal entrance and campsite fee.

Best time to visit: April through October. The temperatures regularly dip below freezing from late October through mid-April. Summer is the most popular time, especially for boating and fishing on the lake.

Activities: Hiking, camping, wildlife observation, archaeology, horseback riding, mountain biking, backpacking, picnicking, boating, fishing, and swimming.

Concessions: Big C's Trading Post offers food, firewood, and other camping supplies. Canoes and paddleboats can be rented during the summer.

Pets: Horses are allowed only in the equestrian areas. Pets must be kept on a leash.

For more information:

Park Superintendent, Caprock Canyons State Park, P.O. Box 204, Quitaque, TX 79255; 806-455-1492.

DINOSAUR VALLEY STATE PARK

More than 120 million years ago in an area southwest of Dallas/ Fort Worth, now Dinosaur Valley State Park, a prehistoric drama took place and was preserved for all time. The place, a jungle-like marsh, shaded by giant palms and frequented by three-foot-long dragonflies; the action, a fifty-foot-long sauropod tears through the trees and across the mudflats, leaving deep imprints, chased by an Acrocanthosaurus, an early ancestor of Tyrannosaurus rex, which also leaves its footprints.

The outcome is unknown, but the event was recorded for all time by the footprints, which told paleontologists the story and which dinosaurs once lived here.

These and other dinosaur prints were discovered here in 1909, in a sleepy gully in the 1,274-acre state park, one of seventeen similar dinosaur sites throughout Texas with identifiable tracks. The last sets of tracks were identified in 1985 when the bones of an iguanodon (a thirty-foot predecessor of modern birds) were discovered in the area.

Many more similar tracks, not fossils but preserved footprints, are probably still hidden in the rock layers. But they are unique because, unlike fossils, they provide clues about the social behavior of the dinosaurs, how they lived, hunted, and moved in herds. Only the recent discoveries of fossilized dinosaur egg nests (found elsewhere in the United States) have provided any additional facts about the lives of the dinosaurs.

The tracks, some up to three feet long, are located along the banks of the Paluxy River, a tributary of the Brazos River. When the dinosaurs walked across these mudflats, they left deep imprints. Within a hundred years, the tracks were probably covered by sedimentary deposits. Gradually the mud turned to stone and the sediment to a softer stone. When the oceans eventually receded and newly formed rivers flowed to the sea, the water eroded the softer stone and exposed the tracks. You can see the tracks from hiking trails that pass nearby.

The interpretive center, near the park entrance on your way into the park, has molded cast replicas of the tracks. Life-sized replicas of a sauropod and a theropod can be seen on the road to the scenic overlook. In 1969, this park was designated a national natural landmark.

Wildlife

Unfortunately, history does repeat itself, in this park at least, where not only dinosaurs but two birds, the black-capped vireo and the golden-cheeked warbler, are almost extinct, despite conservation efforts by park biologists and conservationists. The two species are at the northern edge of their nesting range here in park. A bird checklist is available at park headquarters. Most birders in the park are looking for the vireo and the warbler.

Hiking and Backpacking

Nearly six miles of maintained trails make up the park's Cedar Break Trail System. The main campsites, facilities, and interpretive center are on the river's right bank, while nearly all the trails are on the left bank. There are seven primitive sites for overnight camping, and the trail system leads to three scenic overlooks.

Four main loop trails go into the interior: the River Trail, which leads to several dinosaur track locations and a number of good fishing holes; the Outer Ridge Trail, which is the longest in the park; the Denio Creek Trail; and the short but enjoyable Buckeye Creek Loop. Swimming is allowed in the river, usually a great relief from the heat.

While following the dinosaur tracks you'll probably come across signs of contemporary park residents: coyotes, bobcats, and deer. A trail map is available at the park's entrance and at the interpretive center.

Where: Located southwest of Fort Worth, the park is three miles north of Glen Rose, off FM 205.
Hours: Open daily year-round.
Admission: Nominal entrance and campsite fee.

Best time to visit: The spring and fall months. Summer can be quite hot, and temperatures in winter can drop below freezing.

Activities: Camping, backpacking, picnicking, swimming, fishing, bird-watching, wildlife observation, and dinosaur exhibits at the visitors center. During the summer, evening programs are hosted by the park staff on the weekends.

Pets: Horses allowed on the park trails. Pets must be kept on a leash.

For more information:

Park Superintendent, Dinosaur Valley State Park, Box 396, Glen Rose, TX 76043; 817-897-4588.

COPPER BREAKS STATE PARK

The 1,933-acre Copper Breaks State Park lies near the city of Quanah, near the Oklahoma border. Lake Copper Breaks, with sixty surface acres for boating and swimming, is fed by Devil's Creek, which in turn feeds the Pease River, a tributary of the Red River. The park's topography includes mesas, canyons, winding creeks, and a number of low-grade copper deposits.

History

The park's main claim to fame is that it is near the place where Cynthia Ann Parker was "freed" from her captors, the Comanche Indians. At the age of nine, Cynthia Ann Parker was kidnapped by a raiding party in 1836 near Mexia. During her twenty-four years in captivity she married the Comanche chief, Nocona, adopted Indian customs, and had a son.

But in 1864, a Texas Ranger captain, Sul Ross (for whom Sul Ross University in Alpine, Texas, is named), located and recaptured the then thirty-three-year-old woman. Ten years later, in 1874, her son, Quanah, now the chief of the Comanches, led the tribe against the U.S. Cavalry in the battle at Palo Duro Canyon. According to the story, Cynthia's health failed after her separation from the tribe, and she died soon afterwards.

The visitors center is near the entrance, close to a fenced enclosure for a small herd of Texas longhorn cattle. Exhibits in the center include fossils from the Permian age, a history of the Comanches, and examples of local wildlife, including the buffalo, which once inhabited the park.

According to park rangers, this area of Texas was once prairie grasslands, but extensive farming and overgrazing so depleted the soil that it could no longer support the tall bluestem and grama grasses that had fed antelope and buffalo herds.

Hiking and Horseback Riding

Two hiking trails, shown in a trail guide available at the visitors center, let you explore the park. The first trail, the Juniper Ridge Nature Trail, is a short loop that starts from the south edge of Lake Copper Breaks, on the east shore. The second, the Bull Canyon Hiking Trail, goes into Bull Canyon, the park's only primitive camping area.

To reach this primitive campsite, look for the trailhead, easily visible on the road between the Comanche Camping Area and the scenic overlook. The trail leads south through a wooded canyon, then east to the campsites.

The park is a favorite destination for horseback riding. After passing the headquarters and a series of pyramid-shaped shelters in the Comanche Camping Area, the road continues on to the Big Pond Equestrian Area. Nearly one-third of the park is devoted to horseback riding, and riders are expected to stay on the trails (riding cross-country is not allowed), which start from the cul-de-sac near the Big Pond campsites. A spur of the main loop trail leads around Big Pond to the east shore and then turns north.

Wildlife Observation

Wildlife observation is one of the park's other attractions. Beavers live and build lodges along the lake, creeks, and Big Pond. Bobcats, deer, rabbits, and rodents, all of which have adapted to cattle and man and coexist easily with the construction of the Copper Breaks reservoir, live in the canyons and mesas.

Where: Follow State 6 south from the town of Quanah for thirteen miles to the entrance to the state park.
Hours: Open daily year-round.
Admission: Nominal entrance fee, additional nominal fee for camping.
Best time to visit: April through November. In winter, temperatures can be too cold for camping.
Activities: Hiking, fishing, picnicking, camping, boating (no waterskiing), nature trails, equestrian trails, and backpacking. A well-organized interpretive center provides information on the history and ecology of Copper Breaks. Slide shows are provided by the park staff in the evenings at the amphitheater.
Pets: Allowed only on a leash.
For more information:
    Copper Breaks State Park, Route 2, Box 480, Quanah, TX 79252; 817-839-4331.

CADDO LAKE STATE PARK
AND WILDLIFE MANAGEMENT AREA

Caddo Lake State Park, a small, 480-acre park, is not actually on Caddo Lake. The park is linked to the lake by Big Cypress Creek, which forms a boundary of the park. Originally Caddo Lake was the largest natural lake in Texas, perhaps even the largest lake in all of the southeastern states. Some think the lake might have been formed by an earthquake, others by natural log jams and the accumulation of brush and silt.

However, in 1914, the Army Corps of Engineers built a dam to manage the water levels on the lake. Today the lake stretches across 32,700 acres, and across the border into Louisiana.

History

Originally, the park was created to provide boat access to Caddo Lake, for fishing. Then in 1991, 589 acres of Caddo Lake were sold to the nonprofit Nature Conservancy of Texas to be preserved as a wetlands park for ecotourism, the first time that any portion of the lake had been formally protected as a nature preserve.

In the following year, 1992, the Texas Parks and Wildlife Department purchased 6,445 acres of Caddo Lake wetlands. The Nature Conservancy turned over its acreage to the state, bringing to over 7,000 the number of acres of protected lake wetlands. This newly protected area is now known as the Caddo Lake State Park and Wildlife Management Area. A plan to manage the park for ecotourism was being finalized in 1994.

Caddo Lake and Boating

Cabins were built and campsites established along the shore for weekend vacationers, fishermen, and bird-watchers. A state-constructed boat ramp on Big Cypress Bayou provides waterway access to Caddo Lake and from there to the thousands of acres of swamplands.

Over forty miles of boat paths wind throughout the lake,

where thousands of cypress trees draped in Spanish moss tower over the calm, flat water, their knees rising out of the shallows.

Hiking

For those not interested in boating or fishing, the park staff maintains a three-mile hiking trail and a one-third-mile interpretive nature trail that wind through the park's wetlands areas, where bald cypress trees grow in swamplands. The trailheads for the hiking trail and the interpretive trail are well marked on the main road leading from the park entrance to the boat ramp. Trail guide booklets and trail markers point out plants and vegetation zones.

Wildlife Observation

Bird-watching and nature photography are two of the most popular activities on Caddo Lake and in the park. Though rarely seen, alligators are known to live in the creek and lake, which is also home to over a hundred bird species. Herons, mallards, ducks, and warblers are regular visitors to the area, as is the endangered bald eagle. Bird-watchers can pick up a checklist for the park and the lake from the entrance station.

Mammals are rarely seen because of the park's size, although deer, beaver, and other small animals live in the park and the surrounding forest. Beaver, which stay near the water, are most often seen.

Camping and Accommodations

Visitors to the park can rough it, bring a trailer, or stay in one of the nine rental cabins constructed near the park's recreation hall, playground, and picnic area. Because the cabins are so popular, call ahead for reservations.

There are twenty primitive campsites with water only, and another twenty-eight with electrical and sewage hookups. Some of the campsites lie near Saw Mill Pond, a lagoon off Big Cypress Creek; the rest are nestled into the forest. Three screened shelters provide relief from the mosquitoes and flies, making a visit to Caddo enjoyable even in the hot, humid summer. Swimming is allowed in the pond and bayou. The bayou, boat ramp, and fishing pier are a short walk away. A concessionaire provides canoe rentals from spring through fall, and operates a snack shop.

Where: Fourteen miles east of Marshall on State 43 and FM 143.
Hours: Open daily year-round.
Admission: Nominal entrance and camping fees.
Best time to visit: Year-round, although temperatures in winter sometimes drop below freezing.
Activities: Swimming, picnicking, camping, canoeing, motorboating, hiking, interpretive nature trail, wildlife observation, bird-watching, and fishing.
Concessions: A small store sells snacks and rents canoes.
Pets: Allowed on a leash.
Other: Bring insect repellent during the summer.
For more information:
   Caddo Lake State Park, Route 2, Box 15, Karnak, TX 75661; 214-679-3351.

THE NATIONAL GRASSLANDS OF TEXAS

Four separate National Grasslands in northern Texas, with a total of 117,032 acres, are Rita Blanca and McClellan Creek, in the Texas Panhandle, and Caddo and Lyndon B. Johnson between

Dallas and the Oklahoma border. While no one feature of the Grasslands makes them stand out among Texas parks, they are valuable for their native prairie vegetation and wildlife.

History

In the 1830s, 12 million acres of virgin grasslands in Texas were open to large buffalo and antelope herds, which roamed freely through the region. By the 1930s, the buffalo were nearly extinct and only 5,000 virgin acres remained, the rest having been plowed under for farms or denuded by cattle ranching.

When the depression struck in the early 1930s, the government began to reacquire the land that today comprises the four National Grasslands. The land, however, had been so badly exhausted that most was dried and cracked wasteland, unable to support even weeds.

The process of restoration began, and by the 1950s, 117,032 acres of rehabilitated prairie and mixed woodlands in Texas were designated as National Grasslands. Other grasslands were also established in Colorado, Oklahoma, and Kansas.

Since the National Grasslands were created from tracts of former private land, they are often a patchwork of parcels, separated by private property. If you visit any of the four Grasslands, get a Forest Service map first, in order to avoid trespassing on private property.

Land Management

Aggressive soil conservation efforts have led to widespread revegetation of land once thought beyond repair. The soil conservation efforts expanded in the 1960s to include surface resource management. Reintroduction and the spread of birds and animals throughout the prairie lands marked the resurgence of the environment and the re-creation of nearly original wilderness, except for the buffalo, which have not been reintroduced in the wild.

The U.S. Forest Service's charter is to balance the pressures of environmental protection and resource usage in the National Grasslands. A program of carefully monitored cattle grazing, selective burns, and recreational use is designed for both preservation and selective use.

Recreation

Boating, camping, hiking, and wildlife viewing are all popular activities at the Grasslands. Swimming in the lakes is not prohibited but discouraged, and fishing for bass, catfish, and bream is allowed only as a means of resource management. Most National Grasslands have no developed hiking trails, but you are free to wander anywhere on federal property. There are a very few primitive campsites, but even better, you can pitch your tent wherever you want and pretend you are a pioneer.

With so much open, undeveloped rolling timber and prairie lands, it is not surprising that horseback riding and trail camping in the Grasslands are so popular. Before heading out to the Grasslands, contact the Forest Service rangers to get a map and check local rules and hunting season dates.

Rita Blanca National Grassland

Rita Blanca National Grassland, at 77,463 acres the largest of the four National Grasslands, displays the classic vegetation of Texas's rolling prairie grasslands: long-stem and short-stem grasses, small shrubs, and almost no trees. The park is tucked up into the far northwestern corner of the Panhandle near the Oklahoma–New Mexico border.

Rita Blanca is teaming with pronghorn antelope herds routinely seen grazing or bounding through the grass during daylight hours. The prairies are also covered with prairie dog towns, where dozens of dirt mounds mark the entrances and exits of underground tunnels and rooms. The prairie dogs are food for coyotes and foxes, which emerge at dusk to forage, and for hawks hunting during the day.

During spring and summer, wildflowers burst into bloom. These displays are particularly colorful at the Thompson Grove Recreation Site, notable for Rita Blanca's only thicket of trees and thus a good place to see pheasants, buntings, and other birds.

With so much open space, horseback riding is a great sport, but there are also hiking, mountain biking, and camping. You can pitch a tent anywhere without a camping permit. A network of unimproved roads across parkland makes it possible to car-camp, but four-wheel-drive vehicles are recommended for some roads, especially after a thunderstorm when mud holes develop.

The prairies are an unpleasant place to be in winter, and visitors rarely come during these months. With nothing to break the wind, howling storms and blizzards are not unusual. When spring rolls around and the temperatures rise, horseback riders, campers, and hikers park along the roadways and take advantage of the parklands.

Where: In the far northwest corner of the Panhandle near the Oklahoma border. Take State 296 east from Texline and follow the signs to the Grassland.
Activities: Camping, hiking, horseback riding, picnicking, wildlife observation, and bird-watching.
For more information:
Rita Blanca National Grassland, U.S. Forest Service, P.O. Box 38, Texline, TX 79087; 806-362-4254.

The prairie dog's barking call led to its name

Lyndon B. Johnson National Grassland

The Lyndon B. Johnson National Grassland, north of Fort Worth east off I-81, is the second largest National Grassland in the state with 20,324 acres. Divided into over three dozen separate management units, this preserve's many tracts of land are interspersed with private property. The habitat varies considerably, from flat grasslands to riparian forests, oak timberlands, and lakes.

Most visitors here are birders, who come out to observe the annual waterfowl migration in fall and spring. Identified waterfowl include geese, ducks, cranes, egrets, herons, grebes, and terns. Other animals reportedly seen in the area but rarely spotted are coyotes, foxes, squirrels, deer, and bobcats.

As in the other grasslands, horseback riding is the most popular recreation activity; the broad prairies and dozens of roads are made for riders. Get a Forest Service map so you won't trespass onto private property.

Cattle grazing is permitted during certain times of year, so you may encounter herds. There are no particular restrictions on horse trailers; often horsemen come out in a group and park in a line along the dirt roads. Recently, mountain and road biking have caught on as well.

Although camping is allowed anywhere in the grassland, a primitive campground with seven sites for nonriders—hikers and fishermen—is at the Black Creek Recreation Site, near Black Creek Lake. The lake has a boat ramp, and there are a number of hiking trails in the vicinity. You can also boat nearby on Cottonwood Lake, where there are no camping facilities.

Where: North of Decatur along FM 730. Get a Forest Service map from the district office in Decatur before going.
Activities: Horseback riding, camping, hiking, picnicking, fishing, bird-watching, and wildlife observation.
Other: Owners of private property take a dim view of trespassers.
For more information:
    Caddo and Lyndon B. Johnson National Grasslands, U.S. Forest Service, FM 730 South, Decatur, TX 76234; 817-627-5475.

McClellan Creek National Grassland

The 1,449-acre McClellan Creek National Grassland is the smallest of the four grasslands but famous for the bald eagles that arrive during the winter months. McClellan Creek is adjacent to Black Kettle National Grassland in Oklahoma, and both are managed by the Forest Service office in Cheyenne, Oklahoma. If you come to McClellan Creek, you might want to drive up to Cheyenne and visit Black Kettle as well.

Bird-watchers from across the Panhandle usually visit this area during the fall and spring migrations, which generally last from September through December, and from March to May. Hundreds of bald eagles move through the area, spend time in the grassland, and can easily be seen with binoculars. Various species of ducks, geese, cranes, and egrets arrive by the thousands.

Later in spring the wildflowers bloom, with a spectacular display of bluebonnets, Indian paintbrush, and Indian blankets. Some permanent residents of the grasslands and woodlands are present but seen infrequently, including deer, coyotes, squirrels, rabbits, bobcats, snakes, and turkeys. Bats are common over the lake in the evening, twisting and turning as they hunt for insects.

Other recreation at the grassland is 400-acre McClellan Lake, which has a boat ramp, campsites, and picnic grounds. Swimming is allowed.

Where: Halfway between Amarillo and Shamrock. From I-40 turn on FM 2477 to the National Grassland.
Activities: Camping, bird-watching, boating, picnicking, wildlife observation, swimming, and wildflowers.
For more information:
McClellan Creek National Grassland and Black Kettle National Grassland, U.S. Forest Service, Route 1, Box 55B, Cheyenne, OK 73628; 405-497-2143.

Caddo National Grassland

Most of Caddo National Grassland, 17,700 acres, is not a true grassland but lies in the transition zone between the blackland prairies and the oak savannas. The terrain, therefore, below 1,000 feet in elevation and receiving an average annual rainfall of forty inches, is varied, ranging from lakes to wooded forests and open prairie. The grassland lies near the border with Oklahoma and the Red River.

The habitats vary, too, from blackjack oak savannas to long-stem grasslands, to cedar and pine forest, and support a variety of plants and animals. More than a hundred species of birds have been identified in the area.

Recreation is also varied, with good fishing for bass and catfish, and camping, hiking, and horseback riding. Hunting for deer and birds is allowed, so you may want to avoid visiting during the hunting season.

Although you can camp, hike, and fish anywhere on federal property, two recreation areas have been developed. The Coffee Mill Lake Recreation Area has hiking trails and a 700-acre lake with a ramp for fishing and boating. Swimming is allowed. The campground has thirteen primitive sites with running water. Try bushwhacking if you really want to see the wildlife and get some exercise.

The second recreation area, Lake Davy Crockett, has a 450-acre lake with a boat ramp and a primitive campground with nine sites and running water. Neither campground has RV hookups. The two recreation areas are frequently filled on the weekends from spring through fall.

Where: East of Sherman and north of I-82.
Activities: Boating, horseback riding, picnicking, fishing, camping, swimming, bird-watching, hiking, and wildlife observation.

For more information:

Caddo and Lyndon B. Johnson National Grasslands, U.S. Forest Service, FM 730 South, Decatur, TX 76234; 817-627-5475.

Index

ARCHAEOLOGICAL
ATTRACTIONS
Big Bend Ranch State Natural
Area, 35–40
Caprock Canyons State Park,
141–144
Enchanted Rock State Natural
Area, 2–5
Hueco Tanks State Historical
Park, 49–52
ASTRONOMY
George Observatory, Brazos
Bend State Park, 82
McDonald Observatory,
47–48

BACKPACKING. *See*
HIKING; PRIMITIVE
CAMPING
BEACHCOMBING
Mustang Island State Park,
114–117
Padre Island National
Seashore, 117–122

BICYCLING. *See also*
MOUNTAIN BIKING
Big Bend National Park,
29–35
Big Bend Ranch State Natural
Area, 35–40
Big Thicket National
Preserve, 62–70
Brazos Bend State Park,
78–83
Lost Maples State Natural
Area, 13–16
Lyndon B. Johnson National
Grassland, 156–157
Santa Ana National Wildlife
Refuge, 124–128
BIRD-WATCHING
Anahuac National Wildlife
Refuge, 96–99
Aransas National Wildlife
Refuge, 108–112
Bentsen–Rio Grande Valley
State Park, 128–132
Big Bend National Park,
29–35

Big Thicket National
Preserve, 62–70
Brazoria National Wildlife
Refuge, 105–107
Brazos Bend State Park,
78–83
Caddo Lake State Park and
Wildlife Management
Area, 149–152
Caddo National Grassland,
159–160
Caprock Canyons State Park,
141–144
Davis Mountains State Park,
45–46
Dinosaur Valley State Park,
144–147
Galveston Island State Park,
102–103
Guadalupe Mountains
National Park, 40–44
Hueco Tanks State Historical
Park, 49–52
Inks Lake State Park, 22–25
Laguna Atascosa National
Wildlife Refuge, 122–124
Lost Maples State Natural
Area, 13–16
Lyndon B. Johnson National
Grassland, 156–157
McClellan Creek National
Grassland, 158
McFaddin National Wildlife
Refuge, 95–96

Martin Dies Jr. State Park,
76–78
Mustang Island State Park,
114–117
Palmetto State Park, 8–13
Palo Duro Canyon State
Park, 137–141
Pedernales Falls State Park,
25–27
Rita Blanca National
Grassland, 154–155
Roy E. Larson Sandyland
Sanctuary, 71–74
Sabal Palm Grove Sanctuary,
132–134
San Bernard National
Wildlife Refuge, 107–108
Santa Ana National Wildlife
Refuge, 124–128
Sea Rim State Park, 92–95
BOATING
Alabama-Coushatta Indian
Reservation, 74–76
Anahuac National Wildlife
Refuge, 96–99
Angelina National Forest,
84–85
Bentsen–Rio Grande Valley
State Park, 128–132
Big Thicket National
Preserve, 62–70
Caddo Lake State Park and
Wildlife Management
Area, 147–149

Caddo National Grassland,
  159–160
Caprock Canyons State Park,
  141–144
Copper Breaks State Park,
  147–149
Davy Crockett National
  Forest, 85–86
Inks Lake State Park, 22–25
McClellan Creek National
  Grassland, 158
McFaddin National Wildlife
  Refuge, 95–96
Martin Dies Jr. State Park,
  76–78
Mustang Island State Park,
  114–117
Sabine National Forest,
  86–87
Sam Houston National
  Forest, 87–88
San Bernard National
  Wildlife Refuge, 107–108
Sea Rim State Park, 92–95
Seminole Canyon State
  Historical Park, 56–58
BOTANICAL GARDENS
Moody Gardens, 100–101

CABIN RENTALS
Caddo Lake State Park and
  Wildlife Management
  Area, 149–152

CAMPING. *See also* HORSE
  CAMPING; PRIMITIVE
  CAMPING
Alabama-Coushatta Indian
  Reservation, 74–76
Anahuac National Wildlife
  Refuge, 96–99
Angelina National Forest,
  84–85
Bentsen–Rio Grande Valley
  State Park, 128–132
Big Bend National Park,
  29–35
Big Bend Ranch State Natural
  Area, 35–40
Brazos Bend State Park,
  78–83
Caddo Lake State Park and
  Wildlife Management
  Area, 149–152
Caddo National Grassland,
  159–160
Caprock Canyons State Park,
  141–144
Copper Breaks State Park,
  147–149
Davis Mountains State Park,
  45–46
Davy Crockett National
  Forest, 85–86
Dinosaur Valley State Park,
  144–147
Galveston Island State Park,
  102–103

Guadalupe Mountains
National Park, 40–44
Hill Country State Natural
Area, 6–8
Hueco Tanks State Historical
Park, 49–52
Inks Lake State Park, 22–25
Lost Maples State Natural
Area, 13–16
Lyndon B. Johnson National
Grassland, 156–157
McClellan Creek National
Grassland, 158
McFaddin National Wildlife
Refuge, 95–96
Martin Dies Jr. State Park,
76–78
Monahans Sandhills State
Park, 53–55
Mustang Island State Park,
114–117
Padre Island National
Seashore, 117–122
Palmetto State Park, 8–13
Palo Duro Canyon State
Park, 137–141
Pedernales Falls State Park,
25–27
Rita Blanca National
Grassland, 154–155
Sabine National Forest,
86–87
Sam Houston National
Forest, 87–88

Sea Rim State Park, 92–95
Seminole Canyon State
Historical Park, 56–58
CANOEING
Alabama-Coushatta Indian
Reservation, 74–76
Bentsen–Rio Grande Valley
State Park, 128–132
Big Thicket National
Preserve, 62–70
Caddo Lake State Park and
Wildlife Management
Area, 149–152
Caprock Canyons State Park,
141–144
Davy Crockett National
Forest, 85–86
Palmetto State Park, 8–13
Rio Grande Wild and Scenic
River, 29–35
Roy E. Larson Sandyland
Sanctuary, 71–74
CAVES and CAVERNS
Caverns of Sonora, 18–20
Longhorn Cavern State Park,
20–21
Natural Bridge Caverns, 17–18
Seminole Canyon State
Historical Park, 56–58
Wonder Cave, 21–22
CHILDREN'S and FAMILY
ACTIVITIES. *See also*
EDUCATIONAL
PROGRAMS

Alabama-Coushatta Indian
  Reservation, 74–76
Big Bend Ranch State Natural
  Area, 35–40
Big Thicket National
  Preserve, 62–70
Chihuahuan Desert Research
  Institute, 46–47
Dinosaur Valley State Park,
  144–147
Galveston Island State Park,
  102–103
Moody Gardens, 100–101
Padre Island National
  Seashore, 117–122
Palo Duro Canyon State
  Park, 137–141

DINOSAUR EXHIBITS
Dinosaur Valley State Park,
  144–147

EDUCATIONAL PROGRAMS
Big Bend National Park,
  29–35
Big Bend Ranch State Natural
  Area, 35–40
Big Thicket National
  Preserve, 62–70
Chihuahuan Desert Research
  Institute, 46–47

Padre Island National
  Seashore, 117–122
Palmetto State Park, 8–13

FISHING
Alabama-Coushatta Indian
  Reservation, 74–76
Anahuac National Wildlife
  Refuge, 96–99
Angelina National Forest,
  84–85
Aransas National Wildlife
  Refuge, 108–112
Bentsen–Rio Grande Valley
  State Park, 128–132
Brazoria National Wildlife
  Refuge, 105–107
Brazos Bend State Park,
  78–83
Caddo Lake State Park and
  Wildlife Management
  Area, 149–152
Caddo National Grassland,
  159–160
Caprock Canyons State Park,
  141–144
Copper Breaks State Park,
  147–149
Davy Crockett National
  Forest, 85–86
Dinosaur Valley State Park,
  144–147
Inks Lake State Park, 22–25

Laguna Atascosa National
Wildlife Refuge, 122–124
Lost Maples State Natural
Area, 13–16
Lyndon B. Johnson National
Grassland, 156–157
McFaddin National Wildlife
Refuge, 95–96
Martin Dies Jr. State Park,
76–78
Mustang Island State Park,
114–117
Padre Island National
Seashore, 117–122
Palmetto State Park, 8–13
Pedernales Falls State Park,
25–27
Rio Grande Wild and Scenic
River, 29–35
Sabine National Forest, 86–87
Sam Houston National
Forest, 87–88
San Bernard National
Wildlife Refuge, 107–108
Sea Rim State Park, 92–95

GEOLOGIC ATTRACTIONS.
See also CAVES AND
CAVERNS
Big Bend Ranch State Natural
Area, 35–40
Caprock Canyons State Park,
141–144

Dinosaur Valley State Park,
144–147
Enchanted Rock State Natural
Area, 2–5
Guadalupe Mountains
National Park, 40–44
Hueco Tanks State Historical
Park, 49–52
Monahans Sandhills State
Park, 53–55
Odessa Meteor Crater, 55–56
Palo Duro Canyon State
Park, 137–141
GUIDED TOURS and
WALKS. *See also* TOURS
Caverns of Sonora, 18–20
Hueco Tanks State Historical
Park, 49–52
Longhorn Cavern State Park,
20–21
Natural Bridge Caverns,
17–18
Roy E. Larson Sandyland
Sanctuary, 71–74
Santa Ana National Wildlife
Refuge, 124–128
Seminole Canyon State
Historical Park, 56–58
Wonder Cave, 21–22

HANDICAPPED ACCESS
Beach Unit, Sea Rim State
Park, 93

Hickory Creek Savanna Unit, Big Thicket National Preserve, 65–66

Turkey Creek Unit, Big Thicket National Preserve, 64–65

HIKING. *See also* NATURE TRAILS

Alabama-Coushatta Indian Reservation, 74–76

Anahuac National Wildlife Refuge, 96–99

Angelina National Forest, 84–85

Aransas National Wildlife Refuge, 108–112

Bentsen–Rio Grande Valley State Park, 128–132

Big Bend National Park, 29–35

Big Bend Ranch State Natural Area, 35–40

Big Thicket National Preserve, 62–70

Brazoria National Wildlife Refuge, 105–107

Brazos Bend State Park, 78–83

Caddo Lake State Park and Wildlife Management Area, 149–152

Caddo National Grassland, 159–160

Caprock Canyons State Park, 141–144

Copper Breaks State Park, 147–149

Davis Mountains State Park, 45–46

Davy Crockett National Forest, 85–86

Enchanted Rock State Natural Area, 2–5

Fort Davis National Historic Site, 48–49

Galveston Island State Park, 102–103

Guadalupe Mountains National Park, 40–44

Hill Country State Natural Area, 6–8

Hueco Tanks State Historical Park, 49–52

Inks Lake State Park, 22–25

Laguna Atascosa National Wildlife Refuge, 122–124

Longhorn Cavern State Park, 20–21

Lost Maples State Natural Area, 13–16

Lyndon B. Johnson National Grassland, 156–157

Martin Dies Jr. State Park, 76–78

Monahans Sandhills State Park, 53–55

Padre Island National Seashore, 117–122

Palmetto State Park, 8–13

Palo Duro Canyon State
Park, 137–141
Pedernales Falls State Park,
25–27
Rita Blanca National
Grassland, 154–155
Roy E. Larson Sandyland
Sanctuary, 71–74
Sabine National Forest, 86–87
Sam Houston National
Forest, 87–88
San Bernard National
Wildlife Refuge, 107–108
Santa Ana National Wildlife
Refuge, 124–128
Sea Rim State Park, 92–95
Seminole Canyon State
Historical Park, 56–58
HISTORIC ATTRACTIONS.
See also
ARCHAEOLOGICAL
ATTRACTIONS; INDIAN
PICTOGRAPHS
Fort Davis National Historic
Site, 48–49
Hueco Tanks State Historical
Park, 49–52
Longhorn Cavern State Park,
20–21
HORSEBACK RIDING
Big Bend National Park, 29–35
Big Sandy Creek Unit, Big
Thicket National Preserve,
66

Caddo National Grassland,
159–160
Caprock Canyons State Park,
141–144
Copper Breaks State Park,
147–149
Dinosaur Valley State Park,
144–147
Guadalupe Mountains
National Park, 40–44
Hill Country State Natural
Area, 6–8
Lyndon B. Johnson National
Grassland, 156–157
McClellan Creek National
Grassland, 158
Palo Duro Canyon State
Park, 137–141
Rita Blanca National
Grassland, 154–155
HORSE CAMPING
Caddo National Grassland,
159–160
Caprock Canyons State Park,
141–144
Lyndon B. Johnson National
Grassland, 156–157
McClellan Creek National
Grassland, 158
Rita Blanca National
Grassland, 154–155
HUNTING
Anahuac National Wildlife
Refuge, 96–99

Angelina National Forest,
   84–85
Caddo National Grassland,
   159–160
Davy Crockett National
   Forest, 85–86
Sabine National Forest,
   86–87
Sam Houston National
   Forest, 87–88

INDIAN DANCING
   Alabama-Coushatta Indian
      Reservation, 74–76
INDIAN PICTOGRAPHS
   Hueco Tanks State Historical
      Park, 49–52
   Palo Duro Canyon State
      Park, 137–141
   Seminole Canyon State
      Historical Park, 56–58
INTERPRETIVE CENTERS
   and EXHIBITS
   Aransas National Wildlife
      Refuge, 108–112
   Beach Unit, Sea Rim State
      Park, 93
   Brazos Bend State Park,
      78–83
   Copper Breaks State Park,
      147–149
   Dinosaur Valley State Park,
      144–147

Laguna Atascosa National
   Wildlife Refuge, 122–124
Lost Maples State Natural
   Area, 13–16
Monahans Sandhills State
   Park, 53–55

MOUNTAIN BIKING. *See also*
   BICYCLING
   Anahuac National Wildlife
      Refuge, 96–99
   Big Bend National Park,
      29–35
   Brazos Bend State Park,
      78–83
   Caprock Canyons State Park,
      141–144
   Hill Country State Natural
      Area, 6–8
   Lyndon B. Johnson National
      Grassland, 156–157
   Pedernales Falls State Park,
      25–27
   Rita Blanca National
      Grassland, 154–155
   Sam Houston National
      Forest, 87–88
   San Bernard National
      Wildlife Refuge, 107–108

NATURE TRAILS. *See also*
   HIKING

Aransas National Wildlife
Refuge, 108–112
Beach Unit, Sea Rim State
Park, 93
Bentsen–Rio Grande Valley
State Park, 128–132
Big Bend National Park,
29–35
Big Thicket National
Preserve, 62–70
Brazos Bend State Park,
78–83
Caddo Lake State Park and
Wildlife Management
Area, 149–152
Chihuahuan Desert Research
Institute, 46–47
Copper Breaks State Park,
147–149
Fort Davis National Historic
Site, 48–49
Galveston Island State Park,
102–103
Guadalupe Mountains
National Park, 40–44
Lost Maples State Natural
Area, 13–16
Monahans Sandhills State
Park, 53–55
Palmetto State Park, 8–13
Pedernales Falls State Park,
25–27
Roy E. Larson Sandyland
Sanctuary, 71–74

Sabal Palm Grove Sanctuary,
132–134
Santa Ana National Wildlife
Refuge, 124–128

PHOTOGRAPHY
Aransas National Wildlife
Refuge, 108–112
Bentsen–Rio Grande Valley
State Park, 128–132
Big Bend National Park,
29–35
Caddo Lake State Park and
Wildlife Management
Area, 149–152
Santa Ana National Wildlife
Refuge, 124–128
PICNICKING
Aransas National Wildlife
Refuge, 108–112
Brazos Bend State Park,
78–83
Caddo Lake State Park and
Wildlife Management
Area, 149–152
Caddo National Grassland,
159–160
Caprock Canyons State Park,
141–144
Copper Breaks State Park,
147–149
Davis Mountains State Park,
45–46

Davy Crockett National
Forest, 85–86
Dinosaur Valley State Park,
144–147
Galveston Island State Park,
102–103
Hueco Tanks State Historical
Park, 49–52
Laguna Atascosa National
Wildlife Refuge, 122–124
Longhorn Cavern State Park,
20–21
Lost Maples State Natural
Area, 13–16
Lyndon B. Johnson National
Grassland, 156–157
McClellan Creek National
Grassland, 158
McFaddin National Wildlife
Refuge, 95–96
Padre Island National
Seashore, 117–122
Palmetto State Park, 8–13
Pedernales Falls State Park,
25–27
Rita Blanca National
Grassland, 154–155
Roy E. Larson Sandyland
Sanctuary, 71–74
Sabine National Forest, 86–87
Sam Houston National
Forest, 87–88
Seminole Canyon State
Historical Park, 56–58

PLANT LIFE. *See also* TREES
and FORESTS
Bentsen–Rio Grande Valley
State Park, 128–132
Big Bend National Park, 29–35
Big Thicket National
Preserve, 62–70
Chihuahuan Desert Research
Institute, 46–47
Laguna Atascosa National
Wildlife Refuge, 122–124
Lost Maples State Natural
Area, 13–16
Moody Gardens, 100–101
Palmetto State Park, 8–13
PRIMITIVE CAMPING
Angelina National Forest,
84–85
Big Bend National Park,
29–35
Big Bend Ranch State Natural
Area, 35–40
Big Thicket National
Preserve, 62–70
Caddo National Grassland,
159–160
Caprock Canyons State Park,
141–144
Copper Breaks State Park,
147–149
Davy Crockett National
Forest, 85–86
Dinosaur Valley State Park,
144–147

Enchanted Rock State Natural
  Area, 2–5
Guadalupe Mountains
  National Park, 40–44
Hill Country State Natural
  Area, 6–8
Inks Lake State Park,
  22–25
Lost Maples State Natural
  Area, 13–16
Lyndon B. Johnson National
  Grassland, 156–157
McClellan Creek National
  Grassland, 158
Marshlands Unit, Sea Rim
  State Park, 94
Padre Island National
  Seashore, 117–122
Pedernales Falls State Park,
  25–27
Rita Blanca National
  Grassland, 154–155
Sabine National Forest,
  86–87
Sam Houston National
  Forest, 87–88

RAFTING
Big Bend Ranch State Natural
  Area, 35–40
Palmetto State Park, 8–13
Rio Grande Wild and Scenic
  River, 29–35

ROCK CLIMBING
Enchanted Rock State Natural
  Area, 2–5
Hueco Tanks State Historical
  Park, 49–52

SCENIC DRIVES
Aransas National Wildlife
  Refuge, 108–112
Big Bend National Park,
  29–35
Big Bend Ranch State Natural
  Area, 35–40
Davis Mountains State Park,
  45–46
Palmetto State Park, 8–13
SCUBA DIVING
Flower Gardens, Galveston
  Island, 101–102
Inks Lake State Park,
  22–25
SEASHELL COLLECTING.
  See BEACHCOMBING
SPELUNKING. *See* CAVES
  and CAVERNS
SURFING
Padre Island National
  Seashore, 117–122
SWIMMING
Alabama-Coushatta Indian
  Reservation, 74–76
Angelina National Forest,
  84–85

Beach Unit, Sea Rim State
Park, 92–95
Big Thicket National
Preserve, 62–70
Caddo Lake State Park and
Wildlife Management
Area, 149–152
Caddo National Grassland,
159–160
Caprock Canyons State Park,
141–144
Copper Breaks State Park,
147–149
Davy Crockett National
Forest, 85–86
Dinosaur Valley State Park,
144–147
Galveston Island State Park,
102–103
Lost Maples State Natural
Area, 13–16
McClellan Creek National
Grassland, 158
McFaddin National Wildlife
Refuge, 95–96
Martin Dies Jr. State Park,
76–78
Mustang Island State Park,
114–117
Padre Island National
Seashore, 117–122
Palmetto State Park, 8–13
Pedernales Falls State Park,
25–27

Sabine National Forest,
86–87
Sam Houston National
Forest, 87–88

TOURS. *See also* GUIDED
TOURS and WALKS
Big Bend Ranch State Natural
Area, 35–40
Brazoria National Wildlife
Refuge, 105–107
bus, Alabama-Coushatta
Indian Reservation, 74–76
miniature train, Palo Duro
Canyon State Park,
137–141
TREES and FORESTS
Angelina National Forest,
84–85
Big Thicket National
Preserve, 62–70
Davy Crockett National
Forest, 85–86
Laguna Atascosa National
Wildlife Refuge, 122–124
Lost Maples State Natural
Area, 13–16
Monahans Sandhills State
Park, 53–55
Roy E. Larson Sandyland
Sanctuary, 71–74
Sabal Palm Grove Sanctuary,
132–134

Sabine National Forest,
86–87
Sam Houston National
Forest, 87–88
TUBING. *See* RAFTING

WATERFALLS
Big Bend Ranch State Natural
Area, 35–40
WILDFLOWERS
Davis Mountains State Park,
45–46
McClellan Creek National
Grassland, 158
Rita Blanca National
Grassland, 154–155
Roy E. Larson Sandyland
Sanctuary, 71–74
WILDLIFE OBSERVATION
Anahuac National Wildlife
Refuge, 96–99
Angelina National Forest,
84–85
Aransas National Wildlife
Refuge, 108–112
Bentsen–Rio Grande Valley
State Park, 128–132
Big Bend National Park,
29–35
Big Thicket National
Preserve, 62–70
Brazoria National Wildlife
Refuge, 105–107

Caddo Lake State Park and
Wildlife Management
Area, 149–152
Caddo National Grassland,
159–160
Caprock Canyons State Park,
141–144
Copper Breaks State Park,
147–149
Davis Mountains State Park,
45–46
Davy Crockett National
Forest, 85–86
Dinosaur Valley State Park,
144–147
Enchanted Rock State Natural
Area, 2–5
Guadalupe Mountains
National Park, 40–44
Hill Country State Natural
Area, 6–8
Hueco Tanks State Historical
Park, 49–52
Laguna Atascosa National
Wildlife Refuge,
122–124
Lost Maples State Natural
Area, 13–16
Lyndon B. Johnson National
Grassland, 156–157
McClellan Creek National
Grassland, 158
McFaddin National Wildlife
Refuge, 95–96

Monahans Sandhills State
Park, 53–55
Padre Island National
Seashore, 117–122
Palmetto State Park, 8–13
Palo Duro Canyon State
Park, 137–141
Pedernales Falls State Park,
25–27
Rita Blanca National
Grassland, 154–155
Roy E. Larson Sandyland
Sanctuary, 71–74
Sabine National Forest,
86–87
Sam Houston National
Forest, 87–88
San Bernard National
Wildlife Refuge, 107–108
Santa Ana National Wildlife
Refuge, 124–128
Sea Rim State Park, 92–95
Seminole Canyon State
Historical Park, 56–58

Specific animals
African bees, 83, 125–126
alligators, 70, 78–82, 94, 96,
98, 104, 112
ants, 126, 129
bats, 110–111
giant toad, 129
javelina, 110, 123, 129
mountain lions and other wild
cats, 15, 33, 123
paddlefish, 22
Portuguese men-of-war, 119
sea turtles, 118–119
snakes, 11, 35, 70, 94,104,
112, 129
whooping cranes, 108
WINDSURFING
Beach Unit, Sea Rim State
Park, 93
Mustang Island State Park,
114–117

Titles in the Natural Wonders/Green Guide series:

Natural Wonders of Alaska
Natural Wonders of Connecticut & Rhode Island
Natural Wonders of Florida
Green Guide to Hawaii
Natural Wonders of Idaho
Natural Wonders of Massachusetts
Natural Wonders of Michigan
Natural Wonders of New Hampshire
Natural Wonders of New Jersey
Natural Wonders of New York
Natural Wonders of Ohio
Green Guide to Oregon
Natural Wonders of Southern California
Natural Wonders of Texas
Natural Wonders of Vermont
Natural Wonders of Virginia
Green Guide to Washington
Natural Wonders of Wisconsin

All books are $9.95 at bookstores.
Or order directly from the publisher (add $3.00 shipping and handling for direct orders):

Country Roads Press
P.O. Box 286
Castine, Maine 04421
Toll-free phone number: **800-729-9179**